Living with
GLOCKS

The Complete Guide to the New
Standard in Combat Handguns

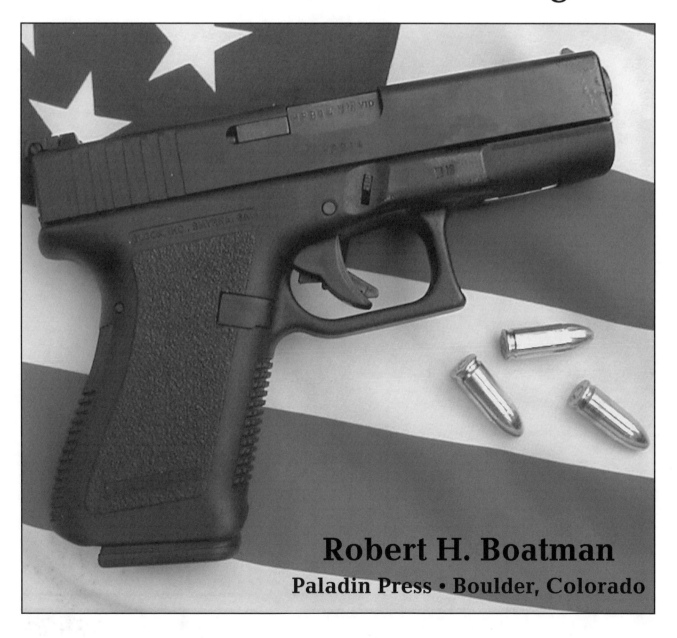

Robert H. Boatman

Paladin Press • Boulder, Colorado

For my father,
breezing along in a yellow convertible
somewhere

Living with Glocks:
The Complete Guide to the New Standard in Combat Handguns
by Robert H. Boatman

Copyright © 2002 by Robert H. Boatman

ISBN 1-58160-340-1
Printed in the United States of America

Published by Paladin Press, a division of
Paladin Enterprises, Inc.
Gunbarrel Tech Center
7077 Winchester Circle
Boulder, Colorado 80301 USA
+1.303.443.7250

Direct inquiries and/or orders to the above address.

Visit our Web site at www.paladin-press.com

Table of Contents

"A strong body makes a strong mind. As to the species of exercises, I advise the gun. While this gives moderate exercise to the body, it gives boldness, enterprise and independence to the mind. Games played with the ball and others of that nature, are too violent for the body and stamp no character on the mind. Let your gun therefore be the constant companion of your walks."

—Thomas Jefferson

"A true Warrior does not seek war, nor does he wish to do battle. He merely believes that it is honorable to cling to a worthy cause. It is noble to reach out to those who are weaker than himself and it is valiant to believe that many things are worth giving up everything for."

— Phil Messina

"Blessed are they who, in the face of death, think only about the front sight."

—Jeff Cooper

Acknowledgments

VERY SPECIAL THANKS

MORGAN W. BOATMAN
for your tolerance, support, and fathomless well of creativity

U.S. CONGRESSMAN HELEN CHENOWETH-HAGE
*for defending the Second Amendment with your heart
and trusting me with your life*

DEAN HESKETH
for teaching me something about being a cop

MAX JOSEPH
for treating me like a Marine and teaching me lessons that changed my life

ALAN ROY
for sticking to your Glocks before it was cool to stick to your Glocks

LLKRWB
for yawning in all the right places

BARCO
wherever you are

And thanks to Chad Hyslop for your earnest enthusiasm and invaluable assistance, Mike Rose for always showing up early and well-armed, Gaston Glock for bestowing upon the world an elegant instrument of personal liberty, Glock shooters worldwide for recognizing excellence when you see it, the National Rifle Association for courage in the face of the enemies of freedom, and Roger Vega for doing your duty in Laos.

First Kiss

1

I kept my first Glock a secret from my closest friends. It was an illicit love affair, as I had practically sworn my faithfulness to the M1911 and felt compelled to conceal my perverted but irresistible temptation to embrace the exotic lightweight polymer, the mind-boggling reliability, the simple reassurance under stress, and the thoroughly unconventional beauty of this new Austrian siren.

I was studying the doctrine of the .45-caliber 1911 pistol hard at the time. Worshipping at the feet of John Browning and Jeff Cooper. Getting my gun handling skills and combat tactics straightened out by Max Joseph, former Recon Marine and head of the Tactical Firearms Training Team (T.F.T.T.) in California.

None of the men I had bonded with in the commitment to large chunks of heavy steel, fat bullets, manual safeties, and Condition One had any suspicion I was simultaneously living in sin with a compact little .40-caliber Glock 23. The secret would not be revealed to them for years.

On the other hand, Max's assistant instructor, Alan Roy, was carrying on with one of these new-fangled toys right out in the open under our very eyes. To make matters even worse, not only was it a plastic gun with a mushy trigger, it fired the decidedly effeminate 9mm Parabellum round.

We all knew of the World War II military reports from a variety of nations that said no less than nine solid hits from a 9mm were required to take an enemy soldier out of action in the heat of battle, and we were not amused. Even though ammunition and especially bullet design had made radical

Legendary Glock shooter, instructor, and competitor Alan Roy recognized the superiority of Glocks immediately. Photo by T.F.T.T.

Max Joseph, head of Tactical Firearms Training Team, has instructed professionals all over the world in both 1911s and Glocks. Photo by T.F.T.T.

Only women, children, and the sociopathically irresponsible went about the world unarmed.

strides forward since the days of hardball, the chilling image of shooting to slide-lock to no avail haunted our minds.

The only firearm more unthinkable was one of those double-action "wondernine" autos designed by lawyers to be used by untrained beginners to shoot in the general vicinity of similarly ill-equipped criminals. At least the Glock certainly was not *that*. One could move back and forth between a single-action auto and a "safe action" Glock easily, though none of us ever said that out loud.

Despite the fact that Alan was a legendary shot and an excellent instructor, he was the constant butt of jokes and target of open derision concerning his odd choice of arms. We all took Alan seriously—he was a Texan and a Marine, after all—but none of us took his Glock 17 seriously. Not in public. Not yet.

Alan accepted our ridicule with good humor. He was no proselytizer, as many Glock converts I've met since have so annoyingly turned out to be. He did not seek to save us from our ancient 1911 sins and enlighten us concerning Glock's advantageous Luger-like grip angle, its low bore axis that resulted in less muzzle flip, its forgiving and indestructible Glock-invented Polymer 2 frame that absorbed tons of recoil while resisting the force of gravity, its fast-to-fire and fast-to-reset trigger, its superior-to-stainless hard-as-a-diamond Tenifer finish, its hard-hitting hammer-forged barrel that actually increased the velocity of jacketed bullets, and its inherent reliability that was part and parcel of Glock's amazingly simple arrangement of less than three dozen component parts. But some of us quietly found all that out on our own.

Sometimes I wondered how many of those Marines, SWAT-team cops, undercover narcs, private bodyguards, between-jobs mercenaries, enthusiastic competitors, and "advanced hobbyists" (to use *Soldier of Fortune*'s

condescending phrase) had, like myself, stashed away a diminutive Glock mistress on the side.

TWO TO TANGO

When I arrived home after a long day at the range, I felt the same excited anticipation mixed with a little guilt that an unfaithful husband feels when he's about to cheat on his wife with a young girl. Or so I've been told.

Off my belt and into the safe went the 2 1/2-pound cocked-and-locked Colt Government Model. After I was properly showered and cologned, I slipped into something more comfortable—my 21-ounce Glock 23 in a thin Galco shoulder holster I had improved immeasurably by taking a sharp pair of leather shears to the politically mandated thumb strap—and luxuriated in my multiple violations of sanctioned faith. Yes, I even had a sip of Scotch to celebrate.

I didn't carry a gun professionally during this time but considered it the most undeniable of adult social responsibilities as I had been taught in my Texas childhood. Only women, children, and the sociopathically irresponsible went about the world unarmed and therefore of piddling use to themselves or any fellow citizen who might find himself or herself in the worst kind of trouble. Private arms are almost always the first and last line of defense—cops arrive on the scene only after the damage wrought by the bad guy has been allowed to happen by shirkers unprepared and incompetent to stop it.

I had also been taught that if you are a person who carries a gun you must be a person who *always* carries a gun, because years of ferocious training can quickly end in terminal embarrassment if you grab your pee-pee at a time when you urgently and unexpectedly need something of a much larger caliber.

But nobody ever said there was anything

wrong with making the commitment to an armed lifestyle as comfortable as possible, so long as you didn't compromise effectiveness by carrying a 9mm or, God forbid, something even smaller that ran the risk of annoying your adversary to the point that somebody (most especially you, not to mention a hapless bystander or two) might get killed. Robert Ruark's admonition to "use enough gun" was spoken out of compassion for the man behind the trigger, not the dangerous animal in front of the muzzle.

The third principle of gun lore I carried in my Texas genes was that if you are going to shoot somebody make sure you shoot him dead, because such action prevents future offenses by the subject in your sights while reducing the pitiful state of overcrowding in our prisons and shrinking the witness list of any self-righteous prosecutor or tort attorney who might try to make you pay a high price for presuming to save your own life.

We should all be aware that, in these days of common narcotics use, the widespread phenomenon of pan-fried brains, and high incidences of psychotic behavior, especially among the young and strong, some individuals under certain conditions can be as hard to kill as a grizzly bear on a drunken rampage.

For all of these reasons and more, I had developed a warm affection for the .40-caliber round accommodated by my G23 and maintain a

Transition from 1911 to Glock is natural. Customized vintage Colt National Match and Glock 36 look different but share spirit and performance. Photo by the author.

close relationship with it to this day, though I consider the .45 ACP modestly superior for defense and the 10mm clearly superior for just about everything else. But these were the days when the only .45-caliber Glock made was the huge first-generation G21, and Winchester's new Black Talon cartridge was promising the first possibility of a near level playing field between medium- and big-bore hollowpoints.

The G23 is the same size in your hand as a compact 9mm, yet it spits out even heavy 180-grain bullets at 1,000 feet per second more or less, producing about the same energy level, and presumably about the same terminal ballistics, as the slower moving 230-grain .45. We used to dig the big .45 Black Talon slugs out of the Los Angeles Yellow Pages after they'd blasted through water jugs to admire their massive and still completely intact flattened shape encircled by all those razor-sharp saw blades we imagined could cut a tree in half as well as a man.

SEA MONSTERS AND OTHER MYTHS

All that talk about flying buzz saws offended the excruciating sensibilities of the hysterical antigun crowd, though not so much as the very name of the cartridge itself. Thus, the pioneering

If you are going to shoot somebody make sure you shoot him dead.

Black Talon went down as the only racist bullet in history, and Winchester finally responded to the gaggle of ignorant crybabies nipping at its heels by renaming the load and restricting its sale to law enforcement agencies only. Apparently, it's okay for a cop to defend his life with the best means available but not for a private citizen to do so. Of course, we all had enough Black Talons stashed away to last for many years. And those vintage boxes are still broken open on occasion to hunt tough game like wild boar or to clear-cut a small forest.

The outrageous myths surrounding the Black Talon cartridge persist to this day among the congenital liars of the antigun crowd and their gullible publics. "Armor-piercing," "cop-killer," and "exploding bullet" are used to describe the very well designed but not radically different Black Talon, which is none of the above.

In the book *American Terrorist* (Regan Books, 2001) there's a passage that reads, "[Timothy McVeigh] was also prepared to use the black Model 21 semiautomatic .45-caliber Glock pistol he was wearing in his shoulder holster. The gun was loaded, and McVeigh was ready to draw the weapon and start firing if he needed to. In the chamber, the handgun had a Black Talon bullet, sometimes known as a cop-killer. Once it penetrates a human body, the Black Talon mushrooms, ripping apart the victim's internal organs."

In fact, for defensive purposes, a new generation of higher-velocity, lighter-weight, faster-expanding bullets soon came along, and those devastating new loads were all given politically correct monikers so as not to over-exercise the pea brains of gun-ignorant journalists and ambulance-chasing representatives of the legal profession.

Winchester Black Talons were beautiful to behold after completing their journeys through water jugs and the L.A. Yellow Pages. We didn't call them flying buzz saws for nothing. Photo by the author.

The first time I took my G23 out in public was a Saturday afternoon aboard the boss' Bertram Sport Fisherman off Newport Beach with some guys I worked with but didn't shoot with. The idea was an informal plinking session using little homemade target-equipped barges, abandoned toy boats, weighted balloons, old basketballs, and other floating crap that belonged at the bottom of the Pacific. Plus any sharks we could chum up.

The armament employed to achieve these lofty goals was a motley assortment of ordinary arms you might find in bedroom closets anywhere in the country—as I recall, there was a lever-action 30-30, a 4-inch Colt .357, a Smith 9mm, a Chinese SKS, some kind of auto-loading 12-gauge, and the boss' chrome-plated marine-model 870 loaded with buckshot. Only when everybody had fired their own and everybody else's guns and the cockpit were ankle-deep in spent shells and the surface of the ocean was clean as new did we return to the harbor.

As proof positive that the Glock appeal is not limited to those who consider the proper selection of a sidearm a potential matter of life and death, two of my office-buddy plinking companions went out the following Monday and bought Glock 23s. I presented each of them with a box of Black Talons and cautioned them not to shoot their kids' leaky basketballs with these explosive, cop-killing, tank-stopping, airplane-downing bullets designed to rip the organs out of unsuspecting victims, decapitate them, and dig a hole and bury them on the spot.

CROSSING STATE LINES

The noose of government oppression was tightening in California, and I left not long after that. Out of sight of the ardent members of my 1911 congregation, I finally did the right thing by my G23, and we became a public item warmly received by my new circle of friends in gun-loving Idaho.

The fact is, Glocks were rapidly becoming the weapon of choice by many, if not yet most, of the law enforcement agencies across the country, from the locals to the feds. And the gun's international reputation as the foremost military sidearm was growing by leaps and bounds. It was now socially acceptable, even among hardheaded SWAT, HRT, and SpecOp types, to be seen with one.

I talked on the phone to my old instructor just the other day, and I must admit that I half-lied to Max, a man to whom it is not easy to lie. He asked if I still shot a 1911 in competition, and I said yes. It wasn't a complete lie, because I do still shoot a 1911 when I compete in IPSC matches. It's just that I hardly ever play that game anymore. On the rare occasions when I shoot strictly for fun nowadays, I mostly shoot less pretentious IDPA matches, and I shoot them with a Glock.

I did admit to Max that I carry a Glock, both professionally and socially, and he did not comment on that. A man of few words who's on record saying that the 1911 is the greatest fighting handgun ever invented, Max did not mention that the contents of his gun safe are by no means limited to American iron these days—a fact I happen to know from other sources.

Neither did Max mention that he was on his way to LAX at the time—on assignment to train elite law enforcement and military forces of a very large South American country in the combat use of Glock pistols. So neither did I go into needless detail about how my professional gun-toting requirements were heating up and I had crucial new needs the lone G23 didn't quite fulfill. I was coming face-to-face with the old adage that says, "If you need to carry a gun, you probably need to carry two."

Besides that, Glock had come out with some sexy new models.

Guarding Helen

2

The first business meeting I had when I moved to Idaho was with a client who, like myself, had been recently transplanted from California. When I saw a signed portrait of Bill Clinton sneering at me from above her desk I knew she would not be my client for long, and I almost turned around then and there to catch the next plane back to the state where at least I was prepared for most of the people I met to be hanging by their teeth on the edge of lunacy.

The second meeting I had in Idaho was also with an escaped Californian. He was a retired LAPD detective who had moved to Idaho for the gun laws, or rather the lack thereof, and for the hunting. He'd traded his department-issue Beretta 9mm for a Glock .45, and we were making our way through the stages of a law enforcement match at the local Boise police range together. When he wasn't outshooting local cops, he carried his Glock in the pocket of his ever-present World War II leather bomber jacket, and he told me he was looking for an elk hunting partner. We became fast friends, and I decided to stay.

The lunatic fringe contingent of California expatriates outnumbered the retired cops—of which there were many—by probably thousands to one and arrived with all of its mutated microbes intact, threatening to infect the innocent native population with vile Left Coast cultural diseases. And that's what led me to become involved in Idaho politics.

As a political consultant, I was equipped to bring an added bonus to my clients. Besides any professional expertise I might have in political strategies, media relations, and mind manipulation, I was also well trained by the aforementioned Max Joseph in VIP protection.

A couple of years earlier, after I had already taken all of the advanced combat shooting courses Max had to offer, and even though I had no ambition to join the Secret Service or become a professional bodyguard, I had decided to devote a few weeks of training to the peculiarly fascinating art of keeping targets alive and well and unshot by other shooters. For reasons that will shortly become clear, I cannot overstate what a good decision that was.

GOOD GUYS, BAD GUYS,
AND WORSE GUYS

In the land of high-profile mavericks like Randy Weaver, Aryan Nations head Richard Butler, government-agent-shooting mountain man Claude Dallas, holocaust-revisionist scholar Michael Hoffman, and retired but hounded LAPD detective Mark Fuhrman and the far more dangerous enemies they attract (hordes of undercover ATF agents and FBI informants, Jewish Defense League terrorist-in-chief Irv Rubin, master scavenger Morris Dees and his Southern Poverty Law Center, radical Marxist activists in the animal-rights and ecology front organizations, various local and vocal crews of chronic protesters and old hippies, relentless racial agitators, and whoever it is manning all those black helicopters), not to mention a sparsely populated community just outside Boise that is a favorite drop-off point in the federal witness protection program, a few of whose free-range criminals have been known to get out of hand, Idaho politicians can sometimes feel a little shaky as they go about meeting and greeting the public in a very friendly state.

The most outspoken, Second-Amendment-defending, loved, and hated of these is U.S. Congressman Helen Chenoweth. Simply put, Helen is a beautiful and graceful lady with solid brass appurtenances the size of bowling balls—highly unusual equipment for any politician regardless of sex. We hit it off immediately.

The first, last, and by far most important

thing you come to terms with in VIP protection is mind-set. In a very real way, bodyguarding is a religious occupation. All of the focus, tactics, and skills you learn in self-defense training are suddenly transformed, as the entire concept of "self" no longer exists. All of the combat capabilities you have mastered in your lifetime are willingly given over in the service of another human being, as often as not a perfect stranger whose total security from so much as a scratched cheek you gladly safeguard with your very life.

Strange perhaps, but nonetheless true. I have never trained or worked with anyone in this discipline who did not immediately and automatically embrace such deliberate and total self-sacrifice. The act of bodyguarding is a powerful and spiritually cleansing phenomenon that conjures the ghosts of mythic heroes who speak in ancient languages to some mystical place in your mind, urging you to kill or be killed in defense of what amounts to a character of your own creation.

Guarding Helen was the same in that mental respect, but substantially different in some physical others. This was not an anonymous business executive who traveled rapidly from one relatively secure location to another. Nor was it some loud-mouthed kid with a guitar whose gravest threat was the hand of a teenage girl clawing out from the crowd to rip open his sequined shirt. It soon became clear to me that political bodyguarding was a peculiar subset of VIP protection doctrine, and I was learning on the job.

The ego of a CEO or a rock star might cause the principal to flaunt the fact that he needs and can afford a bodyguard, thereby intimidating any casual aggressor, but the ego of a politician causes him (or her, in this case) to do the opposite. Adored as she was by many, Helen was a hated figure to an army of mean-spirited left-wing activists who were in and out of town all the time on their various troublemaking missions. Helen was easily accessible (Idaho is a friendly state), instantly recognizable from across a parking lot, and endowed with all the features of a soft, slow-moving target. And she didn't want anyone to know there was a man beside her with a gun.

It soon became clear to me that political bodyguarding was a peculiar subset of VIP protection, and I was learning on the job.

Strolling beside the congressman (one quickly learns not to subvert the English language in the name of political correctness by referring to Helen as a congress*woman* or a congress*person*) on a downtown sidewalk as admiring strangers rushed up and grabbed her was an unsettling experience. As was driving the chase car behind her on an unlit icy road. My first thought was that I was underarmed. The G23 needed support.

MIDNIGHT FANTASIES

With few exceptions, I worked alone so as not to attract undue attention. Thus a rumor started that Helen and I were having an affair, which is not a bad cover story for a covert bodyguard. In any case, I stuck close by her side. And every deadly scenario I could imagine I played out in my head, attaching weapons and tactics to each one.

What if a smiling assassin reached out to greet her with one hand and stab her in the chest with the other? I positioned myself accordingly, playing the odds that the threat would most likely come from a right-handed slasher.

What if the hand extended in friendly greeting suddenly held a handgun? How quickly could I move in front of her? Could I disarm the assailant before taking a disabling shot to the head or chest?

How best to terminate the threat in a crowded room or an outdoor square in the winter with the bad guy bundled up in heavy clothing?

What if the attack followed the armed carjack/kidnap model? I had practiced variations on that one hundreds of times, and it was one of the reasons I preferred shoulder holsters.

A drive-by shooting on a downtown street or a suburban avenue? I would need real firepower for that.

A stray bullet from a faceless crowd? I never knew how extremely suspicious and downright paranoid a person can get, or what mysterious

resources one can draw on to size up a large gathering of people and every individual in it, the slightest furtive glance or movement across the room riveting your attention like a fish nibbling on your bait. There's a reason why the Secret Service loves its sunglasses.

It occurred to me later that one of the reasons I was pretty good at noticing subtle indications of potential threats related to what was also one of the most important lessons I learned in college. Since St. John's in Annapolis was, and is, a pure liberal arts school with no organized sports programs whatsoever, the Naval Academy fencing instructor would walk across the street to give fencing lessons to those of us who were interested. (They let us use the Naval Academy rifle range as well, where I spent considerably more time than in class.) My favorite fencing weapon was the épée because, unlike flailing sabers and fluttering foils, the épée is a real sword, and the rules of engagement in competition are necessarily realistic. In épée fencing, the entire body is the target and the first touch wins, matches often ending with a stab to a wrist exposed for a split-second as an attack is contemplated or a toe extended a fraction of an inch too far forward in anticipation of a lunge.

We used to have midnight matches for which we would remove the hard rubber tips from the ends of the blades and sharpen the points. First blood won, just as in the days when honor was a man's first priority. We soon learned that the slightest telegraphing twitch resulted in immediate bloodshed. The best épée fencers could read minds. They would all have made good bodyguards.

Nothing I've done in my life—not driving open-wheeled race cars at 160 miles an hour two inches from a concrete wall or stalking Rocky Mountain Elk in a blinding snowstorm or wrestling the wheel of an ocean sailing yacht in gale-force winds or even playing high-stakes five-

Flanked by U.S. Congressman Helen Chenoweth (R-ID) and Speaker of the House of Representatives Newt Gingrich (R-GA), the author is discreetly armed with two .40-caliber Glock 27s and a .40-caliber Glock 23 with a spare 30-round magazine, a 10mm Glock 29, a Spyderco Endura, and two automatic knives. Photo by Dan Kimble.

card stud with strangers in the back room of a New Orleans saloon—ever got my juices flowing like guarding Helen. From my motorcycle-racing father I learned a certain personal enthusiasm for danger, but I didn't learn the first thing about keeping other people out of it. From Max I learned a lot about protecting people, but protecting Helen was a new chapter in the lesson book that I would have to write myself.

My tactical solutions may have been over the top, but they made me feel like I was doing my job. It was not going to be *me* standing by

helplessly while one of the great defenders of liberty in the United States Congress was gunned down by a subversive psychopath!

AN ABUNDANCE OF ARMS

My son had recently sent me a beautiful handmade Italian stiletto switchblade, which I have carried in my pocket ever since. Benchmade had come out with a strong little switchblade (automatic knives are legal in Idaho, not that it would have mattered if they weren't) that fit nicely clipped in my waistband in a crossdraw position. And, of course, there was the ever-present Spyderco Endura clipped under my belt. I even bought a black-bladed Spyderco Delica for Helen to carry in her purse, and I made her practice with it until she could flick that serrated edge open like a pro despite her long manicured nails.

I took the G23 out of its shoulder holster and stuffed it down my pants in a Thunderwear rig on the theory that anybody who stares at your crotch long enough and closely enough to figure out that you've got a gun in there is probably not a serious threat, at least not the kind that requires armed response. The G23 was loaded up with 180-grain Black Talons because that's what it had so delightfully digested all its life and there was no reason to change its diet now.

Over my shoulders went a new Galco Miami double rig with two new Trijicon-sighted subcompact Glock 27s, one firmed up under each armpit. (I had fallen in love with the new little Glocks and went out and bought a couple of handfuls of them.) The primary G27 under my left arm carried a magazine full of MagSafe SWAT loads, and I removed the safety strap from the holster for unimpeded access. The G27 under my right arm was loaded with 135-grain Triton Quik-Shoks, and I left the safety strap in place to secure the backup gun in case of a struggle, car crash, or other violent activity. On my belt over my left kidney was a spare 30-round magazine, which of course fit all of the .40-caliber Glocks, loaded with 150-grain Cor Bons. I figured to start with the frangible MagSafes and Quik-Shoks in a close-quarters situation and, if range or multiple-assailant resistance increased, move to the Black Talons and Cor Bons.

In case the bad guys were wearing Kevlar or protected by their car door or windshield or speeding away as they fired, I carried behind my right hip a new compact 10mm Glock 29 loaded with some of the original 200-grain 1200 fps Norma solids I'd paid a premium for at a gun show.

Between the front seats of my 4-door sedan I mounted my trusty competition 12-gauge, a Remington 870 customized by Scattergun Technologies, with buckshot in the extended magazine and rifled slugs in the sidesaddle. And on the inside of the trunk lid I rigged a place for my Bushmaster AR-15 and plenty of spare 30-round magazines.

Go ahead and laugh. I was prepared. In fact, if budget had not been a consideration, I would have replaced the AR-15 with an M16, and mounted a full-auto MAC-10 on my windshield visor. And if Ronald Reagan had not disappointed us all by signing that disastrous 1986 bill outlawing civilian ownership of newly manufactured full autos, a Glock 18 would have been far preferable to the MAC.

Notwithstanding all the extra armament, backups, extended capabilities, and redundant systems, the two most important changes I made in my new steel and plastic wardrobe were the switch from the compact G23 to the subcompact G27 as primary and my first embrace of the 10mm.

It was obvious the Glock 26/27 was a brilliant design from the moment rumors first began to circulate about its imminent introduction. Handgunners had been hooked on high-capacity pistols since the Browning Hi-Power, and Glock had filled that bill superbly, but now America's Clintonista government declared that its "ordinary citizens" should be denied the safety margin of backup rounds.

Gun people can't stand the idea of waste. A big fat service pistol designed for 15- or 18-round magazines unnaturally handicapped by deliberately plugging up the magazines to

It was not going to be me standing by helplessly while one of the great defenders of liberty in the United States Congress was gunned down by a subversive psychopath!

artificially limit capacity is offensive to the aesthetic sensibilities of shooters and anyone else with an iota of appreciation for elegant and organic design. Guns should be, and always had been, designed like airplanes—for maximum efficiency, form following function to produce high-performance mechanisms of inherent beauty.

Gaston Glock agreed. Starting with the given requirement for a 10-round magazine, Glock designed a pistol around it that pushed the envelope for concealable firepower. The same little fighter-jet frame accommodated ladies and Europeans with 10+1 rounds of 9mm and the rest of us with 9+1 rounds of the far more efficient .40 with its unprecedented size-to-power ratio.

He did the same with the .40's mother round, the powerful 10mm brainchild of Jeff Cooper, in the compact G29. The Glock 29 is a substantial step up from the 9mm/.40 in frame size, but it's as small as you can get to reliably handle the longer cases and through-the-roof operating pressures of full-power 10mm loads. Relentless slide battering cracked the steel of the original Dornaus and Dixon Bren Tens as well as heavy Colts and other 1911 frames chambered for the round, and beefed-up Smiths provided to the FBI shot themselves apart in no time. Not so the plastic Glock, which just kept going and going.

THE LESSON OF MIAMI

What a quick and quirky evolution of ammunition. As you all know by now, the FBI adopted the 10mm in response to the infamous Miami shootout of April 11, 1986. "The FBI/Miami Firefight," as the FBI calls it, or "The FBI Massacre," as it's more accurately described, is the most famous shootout since the Gunfight at the O.K. Corral. People who carry guns for a living are still sifting through its ashes for clues to further their future survival.

What happened was that six highly trained FBI agents went up against two highly trained and well-armed killers. Three of the FBI agents were SWAT-qualified, one acclaimed as the best

shot in the Miami field office. The two bad guys were professional criminals, former military police in the 101st Airborne and Rangers who, when they weren't robbing armored cars and banks, tore up the Everglades with about a thousand training rounds every week.

The six FBI agents were armed with 9mm Smith & Wesson 459s and .38 Special Model 19s and J-frames. The two bad guys preferred a fast-handling .223 rifle, a 12-gauge shotgun, and a .357 Magnum revolver. After the initial Chinese firedrill felony car stop, which saw the FBI's top marksman, who was half blind, lose his glasses and two more agents lose their primary guns in the initial impact, the intensive four-minute shootout began.

Before the two criminals were finally killed, two FBI agents lay dead and the other four were gravely wounded. The FBI had fired a verified 70 rounds to score the 18 good hits required to end the fight. The head of the FBI Firearms Training Unit later said, "All else aside, Miami was an ammo failure." Thus the death knell was sounded for 9mm and .38 Special guns in serious law enforcement circles.

Miami and other calamitous experiences with lesser rounds that left FBI agents and other cops strewn around the countryside holding empty .38s and 9mms in their cold dead hands led inexorably to the powerful 10mm round. But, as it turned out, the new smaller Special Agents of the new larger Bureau couldn't control the recoil of the 10mm or the two-handed grips of the large-frame Smith & Wesson 1076s that chambered it. A cartridge that's so good at cracking steel handgun frames is bound to crack a few wrists along the way.

By the time the 10mm was loaded down enough for limper wrists to handle, you could have sawed a large part of the brass case off and put it in a smaller frame. Which is what they did. Thus the .40 was born. And the original superb 10mm was relegated to more serious handgunners mostly west of the Mississippi (and in south Florida), where it remains highly popular and exceedingly useful.

Depending on your choice of bullet weight

and design, the full-power 10mm can stop a car or a grizzly bear, hammer through a windshield, and blow up two bad guys at once—all useful capabilities for a lone bodyguard working without the benefit of teammates equipped with rifles and submachine guns. The most powerful weapons in the world, however, cannot compensate for smaller-caliber minds.

MOUNTAIN TEMPESTS

It was a credible if anonymous rumor of violence and death, and every major politician in the state was gathered together rubbing elbows with every major financial supporter in the state in the 10-ring of the soft target of a jovial primary election night celebration.

The Aryan Nations up in Hayden Lake was gearing up for a larger-than-ever march through the streets of Coeur d'Alene, the JDL was in town from L.A. organizing gangs of protesters, the city council and mayor were threatening to suspend First Amendment rights and, since Idaho's national-level politicians had refused to interject themselves on either side, somebody on one side or the other had apparently noted within earshot of an informer that on this particular night it would be a fairly simple matter to take all those political fence-sitters out at once.

So the Idaho State Police stepped in and took control. They gathered up both congressmen, including Helen, both senators, the retiring governor, and the governor-to-be, along with everybody's senior staff, and ushered them all into a smallish conference room in the hotel for their own protection. The state cops sat there with them and held their hands.

The trouble was, the room they chose as safe

haven for the targets was on the ground floor of the building and featured three entire walls of windows looking out onto a vast and very dark parking lot. You read right.

By the time someone had figured out it might be a good idea to at least close the drapes, three hastily recruited volunteers and I were out in that freezing parking lot cursing the misguided politicians who had made up-to-date fully automatic weapons impossible to legally obtain. Thankfully, the night passed without incident.

And then there were all those Lincoln Day breakfasts, lunches, and dinners. As an unreconstructed Southerner with at least one great-grandfather buried in the Confederate Soldiers' Cemetery in Austin, I have never held that dog-faced son-of-a-bitch in any but the lowest esteem, but northern and western Republicans are proud to be "the party of Lincoln," and they use the Yankee tyrant's birthday as an excuse every year to hold fund-raisers all across the country, during which I keep a straight face and my hand wrapped around a warm Glock.

Having learned to bear it, if not to grin during those occasions, I sometimes recalled the frustration explained to me by friends in California who were bodyguards of candidate Bill Clinton and hundreds of his Hollywood supporters at the notorious fund-raising party in L.A. hosted by Barbra Streisand. I've never met a left-wing bodyguard, and the opportunity to so quickly and easily change the course of history (not to mention the entertainment industry) rarely presents itself.

I remained by the side of Helen Chenoweth through all seasons, from the black-tie Governor's Ball to casual Veterans Day barbecues

The full-power 10mm can stop a car or a grizzly bear, hammer through a windshield, and blow up two bad guys at once—all useful capabilities for a lone bodyguard working without the benefit of teammates equipped with rifles and submachine guns.

The author was fully prepared for his role as bodyguard to such political notables as Lt. Col. Oliver North, J.C. Watts, Don Young and Dick Armey. Photo by the author.

and Western street parades. I learned that a brace of G27s in a good shoulder rig goes unsuspected beneath an unbuttoned tuxedo jacket even when you're shaking hands with the head of the state police, and that a black holster worn over a black T-shirt is easily concealed by even an open white cotton or thin silk outer shirt, and that there is no way not to look foolish when you're walking Secret-Service-style beside your principal who's waving not from the back of a black limousine but from the saddle of a big backcountry mule.

I learned to check for bombs and find electronic bugs. And, when not guarding Helen or performing my other duties as a strategic communications consultant, I helped out with visiting politicos—secretly willing to jump in front

of bullets and open fire on anyone reaching for a weapon in the presence of Newt Gingrich, Ollie North, J.C. Watts, Don Young, Dick Armey, and a host of less illustrious leaders of the free world.

Guarding Helen changed my viewpoint on a lot of things, not the least of which was the concept of competition. I'd shot IPSC for years—against tough competitors in California, Nevada, and Idaho—and I'd more recently taken up IDPA because of its more tactical orientation. But these games, and they are indeed games, began to lose much of their appeal for me. I saw them as marginally useful for some kinds of training, worse than useless for others.

In political bodyguarding, you've got to be prepared to stand up straight and shoot with one hand—not with both hands but with one hand or the other. If you get into any kind of a crouch, the suddenly unprotected principal behind you can take one in the head, and if you don't use your offside arm to shield or shove him (or her) out of the way, he (or she) can quickly become dead meat. You may recall that Ronald Reagan's Secret Service bodyguards inadvertently shoved the president directly into the path of Hinckley's ricocheting bullet. And since we now know that your gun-wielding hand is the most compelling target shining in your adversary's subconscious mind, you'd better be prepared to grab that backup Glock with your weak hand immediately after your strong hand is blown off.

Notwithstanding the highly useful and pioneering Modern Technique of the Pistol, one of the most important forms of training remains the good, old-fashioned, untrendy, boring as hell to hot-doggers, hardly ever shot anymore, strictly disciplined, conventional, fundamental marksmanship you only learn from straight-stance, one-handed, iron-sighted bull's-eye shooting. Before we knew better, that's how we all used to shoot.

Guarding Helen taught me things I had long forgotten as well as things I had never known before. And my loss of boyhood innocence in the joy of competitive shooting was only one of the reasons suiting up with my buddies at the range would never be quite the same again.

Training vs. Competition

3

Competing with your Glock is not the same as training with your Glock. Even if you live for competition, you can die from lack of training. And the best training is of little use if you leave it at the range and don't take it home with you to integrate into your every waking moment. Here's a scenario you might want to think about:

You shot the best match of your life yesterday. Third in your class. All A- and B-zone hits. No dead hostages. Smooth, fast reloads on the run. Your confidence was overflowing. You were so high on victory you even cleaned all of your guns last night.

Now it's today and you're getting dressed. You've got a business meeting this afternoon, and you might want to lose your jacket so maybe you'll stick your carry gun in your pocket holster instead of your usual strong-side IWB. You're just getting out of your car at work when a thought flashes across your mind—you did reload your magazines and chamber a round after you cleaned your carry gun last night, didn't you? You'll check later.

After your meeting, you stop by the ATM to pick up some cash. Suddenly you've got a companion who wants to pick up your cash instead. His pin number is .38. You have every right to draw your weapon and pull the trigger, which you eventually do after slapping at your hip several times and clawing around at every place on your body you've ever carried a gun before.

Finally finding your gun in your hands and knowing that by all rights you should be dead by now, you desperately thrust it out in front of you, knocking your close companion out of your line of fire and staring over your sights at a milling clump of people gathered on the other side of the street to watch you and your predicament. You've got to do something right now even if it's wrong, so you yank the trigger anyway. The massed human flesh across the street doesn't know you're trying to shoot it, so it doesn't scatter for cover. Fortunately, even though you're pulling on the trigger as hard as you can, nothing happens.

Rapidly losing all control of your faculties now, you search for the spare magazine that belongs on your belt but is buried in some pocket somewhere, bring it out in a cloud of lint, and try your best to slam it into the magazine well along with the other empty magazine currently occupying the space. After several hopeless attempts the nature of the problem finally dawns on you and you somehow find the magazine release button (which is a hell of a lot smaller than the one on your competition gun), accomplish a not-so-swift reload, and pull for all you're worth on a trigger that has not been reset. Having no earthly idea why your gun is not firing, your hands take over for your useless mind and execute a tap, rack, slide-lock. No bang.

Your unwelcome ATM companion, who up to this point has been amused by your comical behavior, finally realizes you're trying your best to kill him and turns ugly. He slowly pulls back the rusty hammer of the revolver he stole from a parked car yesterday at about the same time you were bursting with pride at having four pepper

Even if you live for competition, you can die from lack of training. Photo by T.F.T.T.

poppers falling simultaneously, and plants one between your eyes.

Hopefully, you wake up screaming.

If you think you will remain calm and rational when your life is threatened, if you think you will remember all the gunfight doctrine you've read about and casually practiced once or twice, you're lying to yourself in the most dangerous way possible.

RULE NUMBER ONE

The most fundamental and absolute truism in defensive shooting is that, under the crushing mental pressure of a shootout, you will act the way you have trained. As it has been put so eloquently (original source undetermined, but both Clint Smith of Thunder Ranch and Bennie Cooley Jr. of Crisis Resolution Training Consultants say it often), *"In a crisis, you will not rise to the occasion but rather default to your level of training."*

You will not figure out a magical new way to dodge bullets. You will not suddenly innovate a new experimental self-defense system. You will not devise clever new tactics to devastate your attacker. Your mind will not choose this time to blossom into creativity. *You will default to your level of training.* This is true if for no other reason than the inescapable fact that your mind, already supercharged and overrevving to the verge of bending camshafts and blowing heads, will not have any spare horsepower left to override whatever muscle memory you have programmed into your body.

Rule Number One: In a crisis, you will not rise to the occasion but rather default to your level of training.

Even in friendly competition, your IQ drops 15 or 20 points. When you're in the cockpit under fire, it drops at least 30 or 40 points. That's a good thing to keep in mind, if your IQ is currently up to it.

Shooting for score against your friends in the various gun games can rapidly put you on more intimate terms with your sidearm, give you the opportunity to practice proper procedures and gun-handling skills under pressure, improve the timing of your draw and your double-taps, increase your overall shooting speed, and even enhance your marksmanship. It can also ingrain in your mind and muscle memory some awful habits that, in the real world, can get you and those around you shot to death.

Approach competition with caution. Better yet, approach it with a dedicated purpose that has nothing to do with bringing home trophies and winning side bets from overly eager competitors who've sat through too many old Westerns and Hollywood cop movies.

Best of all, take your competition money (if you shoot anything but a Glock, it will cost you several thousands dollars to make your out-of-the-box gun competitive anyway) and invest it in life insurance—ongoing refresher courses and advanced tactical training at Gunsite, T.F.T.T. Thunder Ranch, or any of the other good shooting schools around the country. The best are all run and manned by U.S. Marines, by the way, because there's no such thing as an ex-Marine and because Marines have a hard-core reverence for small-arms know-how in their DNA.

A Marine looking over your shoulder assessing your every move with a cold and unforgiving eye will teach you more in a day than you'll ever learn surrounded by a bunch of jolly competitors just waiting for their turn in the shooting box and hoping you'll shoot yourself in the foot in the meantime.

Competition is a game. Carrying a gun in anticipation of someday using it to resolve a life-and-death situation is not a game. It's never a good idea to confuse the two.

TWO SCHOOLS OF THOUGHT

Even among addicted competitors there are two warring contingents, the "gamesmen" vs. the "martial artists." The gamesmen would just as soon spend their weekends playing a simulated electronic arcade game, and we would all be better off if they would do exactly that. The skills practiced by gamesmen—along with their cousins the single-action quick-draw artists and circus-act trick shots and a lot of "cowboy action" shooters—are, for the most part, wholly irrelevant, impractical, and dangerous as training whether they are intended to be training or not. Such pastimes have little to do with the practical and tactical use of firearms.

Gamesmen could be described as the catch-and-release fishermen of the shooting world because they might as well be firing squib loads or blanks, which, in fact, many of them do. And that's also why a lot of these sport shooters, including many skeet and trap aficionados of my acquaintance, believe it's perfectly okay for *real* guns to be subjected to oppressive government regulations and even banned.

"They'll never ban my $12,000 Perazzi." "They'll never ban my Colt single-action reproduction." "They'll never ban my good-for-nothing-else race gun." Well, in California they even banned Olympic pistols before that particular gun-ignorant law was modified after a lot of pain and heartbreak. Don't trust an eager-beaver gamesman. Don't even shoot with one. They tend to be dangerously soft in the middle.

Way too many "martial artists" are not a hell of a lot better. Granted, these guys take shooting far more seriously than the gamesmen, and they're better at standing up for their rights. But what they practice is still a highly stylized sport that bears as much resemblance to an armed encounter as a boxing match does to a street fight. The highly refined skills of accomplished martial artists can be devastating, but only if their opponents play by the same set of rules, which, as any child will tell you, is never the case.

Another common problem with competition—and this is a problem as well in even the best of training institutes—is that equipment selection and shooting techniques must be restricted in the name of safety. When you've got a bunch of guys firing real bullets, you'd better make damn sure all that lead flies downrange.

Uniform muzzle control in the competitive or training environment must take precedence over the instillation of life-saving skills. Thus such arguable universals as the exclusive use of the strong-side belt holster. This rig is not hallowed because it's necessarily the most effective, but because it's the only kind that's safe to train with *en masse*.

IN PRAISE OF SHOULDER HOLSTERS

I'm a big fan of shoulder holsters for a lot of good reasons—namely concealability, comfort, accessibility, security, convenience, and versatility during the course of normal daily activities like sitting, driving, moving through crowds, and using public facilities.

I don't particularly like anything trying to pull my pants down all day unless it has a prettier smile than a big-bore pistol. But I freely admit that drawing from a shoulder holster on a crowded shooting range will not win you any friends and is far more likely to win you a few enemies for life. And that's the only reason a lot of otherwise sensible firearms instructors go out of their way to denigrate even the modern horizontal (or "transverse," for jargon-inclined academics) shoulder configuration as a specialty or "novelty" carry mode in the same category as ankle holsters. In reality, it's one of only two real advances in gun-wearing technology since very thin and otherwise supple cowhide and horsehide

was first wet-molded and form-fitted. (The other advance is Kydex, which we'll get to in the chapter on holsters.)

The daily life of an instructor does not revolve around shooting bad guys. It revolves around not getting shot with a large-caliber bullet at extremely close range by an accident-prone student. (I remember during one Spyderco class, three fingers of the instructor's hand were very nearly amputated by such a student. Thereafter, we all practiced with sticks.)

Even in Hollywood's favorite days of heavy leather gun pouches worn on wide leather belts to carry big single-action revolvers, it didn't take long for full-time gun wearers in the real world of that time to figure out that hanging their gun pouches under their armpits made the six-gun more comfortable and accessible while sitting at a poker table, not to mention the fact that such a carry prevented the sheriff from snatching their armament from behind while they stood at the bar drinking sarsaparilla, or that it was easier to reach under an arm than behind a hip if some wild-eyed sheepherder knocked them on their butt before they'd made the decision to draw. Things haven't changed much.

Shoulder holsters, worn openly or concealed under roomy coats, were practical and popular for the big revolvers of the past, from about the 1870s on. Today, very similar vertical rigs are widely used for long-barreled hunting handguns in the field. And the form-fitted horizontal rigs for modern compact semiautomatics are highly regarded by the people who actually wear them under their jackets every day.

Shoulder holsters are also a good idea for women, whose high waists preclude any but the most awkward draw from a belt. Just make sure you adjust the shoulder holster to hang a little lower (or a little higher) than anything else that may be hanging from your chest.

For years, manufacturers kept chopping the barrels of their guns shorter and shorter in attempts to make them more concealable. But it's not the barrel that's hard to conceal on a handgun, it's the grip. By aligning the grip with the body under the arm, the horizontal shoulder

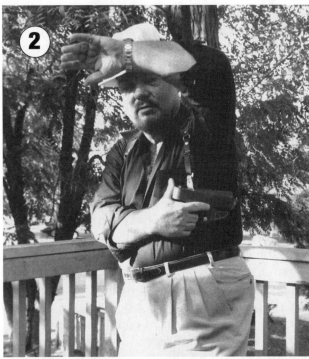

Author demonstrates shoulder holster draw doctrine:

1. Strong-side leg steps back as off-side arm rises in a block.
2. This arm movement clears off-side arm from muzzle sweep and also helps to open unbuttoned jacket and swing horizontally holstered gun into strong hand.
3. Pistol is drawn close across the chest. This quickly puts gun on target, aids retention, and minimizes muzzle sweep of bystanders. The gun can be fired from this position, or . . .
4. Thrust gun hand out to meet off-side hand for two-handed grip in Weaver stance and fire. Note that the draw is not complete until you fire the gun. Photos by Morgan W. Boatman

holster solves that problem handily for every handgun that doesn't have a barrel so long it sticks out the back of your jacket. A hand-filling G23 or G36 is every bit as concealable as a stubby G27 in such a rig.

But don't show up with a shoulder holster at any kind of organized shooting competition or course of instruction. The hotshots who have to hold their guns in their high-tech holsters with their hands will laugh at you, and the range officer or instructor will ask you to leave.

If you make a conscious effort to severely limit the bad habits you're exposed to in competition and develop your own venue to learn the good habits competition doesn't allow, you can overcome the potentially grim pitfalls inherent in shooting for fun. And if you can afford to hire a guru for one-on-one instruction, or if you and a couple of buddies form a very small and very serious training unit, you can get around child-proof safety precautions that can stunt the growth of your life-saving skills.

LESSON NUMBER ONE

In any competitive scenario, by far the most valuable lesson you'll learn is operating your handgun under pressure. This is especially true in the most advanced action shooting sports, IPSC and IDPA.

When you step into the shooting box, there is a Range Officer (RO) standing close behind you barking orders and holding an electronic timer with a very loud buzzer to register your pitiful lack of speed. The RO's free arm is positioned in anticipation of grabbing your gun hand when you make a stupid mistake that could endanger someone's life.

As you move quickly through the course, the RO is at your heels, chasing you, ready to tackle you like an escaping armed criminal at any moment. During all of this, the eyes of fifty or a hundred similarly armed men are watching you. They temporarily despise you and secretly pray you'll screw up, catastrophically or even tragically.

When the run is over, the Range Officer yells out your time, and other men descend upon your targets, searching out misses and poor hits, which they announce for everyone to hear. You're quickly sized up by every man within earshot, either written off as a hopeless and probably dangerous incompetent or targeted as some kind of jackass show-off who must be taught a lesson.

The pressure is hard to ignore completely and, for more excitable types, can be quite difficult to deal with. How often have you seen an otherwise practiced shooter draw on a big steel pepper popper and—for all the world to see—miss with the first shot, take careful aim and miss with the second shot, and, as nerves coil tighter and adrenaline-fueled hands begin to shake and trigger finger grows weak and numb, tumble into a "spray and pray" mode and empty an entire high-capacity magazine to no more effect than raising puffs of dust around that contemptuous silhouette which, if it had been an armed criminal, would have killed the unstrung shooter a dozen times over?

For a man with a gun, public humiliation in front of his peers can be as great a fear as losing a real gunfight. That's why so many promising shooters refuse to compete. They do so to their own detriment. Because, despite its limitations, facing and overcoming the fear of humiliation in competition will eventually build the kind of confidence that will steady you when you're facing not steel and paper but flesh and blood.

Competition has an important place in a well-rounded training regimen, just so long as you know what you can gain by competing and what you can't. And just so long as you don't allow yourself to pay the too-high price of becoming distracted by a pointless desire to win the game.

The best training puts you under heavy pressure to do things properly and also applies competitive pressure to do the proper things better and faster than you thought you could.

You learn from mistakes, not from good luck. Training and competition pressure you to make your mistakes in a controlled environment, where the price if not the intensity of each lesson is

There are potentially grim pitfalls inherent in shooting for fun.

greatly reduced. In shooting, you seldom make the same mistake twice.

THE MODERN TECHNIQUE, THE M1911, AND JEFF COOPER

Every legitimate firearms training academy is based on the same solid foundation—the Modern Technique of the Pistol. Now accepted military and police doctrine, it was originally perfected, documented, and taught by Col. Jeff Cooper (USMC, ret.) and friends on their own time for their own purposes and implemented on the platform of John Browning's .45-caliber M1911 semiautomatic pistol. Accept that without question.

No matter how many Glocks you currently have under your jacket and in your safe, buy yourself a Colt or Springfield Armory or Kimber 1911 and take it to school. It's the best training for operating your Glocks you'll ever get. Even if your chief instructor says it's okay to go through a course with your Glock (all will cheerfully accept Glocks in class these days), it's a good idea to start your formal training with a 1911 because there are universal defensive handgun truths that were born in this pistol and continue to live their most vivid lives within its slab-sided soul. The things you'll learn with a 1911 in your hands are things you need to know. Later, you'll happily discover that your state-of-the-art Glock is far more spiritually akin to your out-of-date 1911 than you might have imagined.

One thing very definitely not to bring to school is a double-action auto of any sort whatsoever. No fancy Walthers or SIGs, no complicated H&Ks or clunky Rugers. None of those odd contraptions Jeff Cooper dubbed "crunchentickers" because of the disturbing difference in both grip and trigger pull between first and follow-up shots. Even if you're a modern soldier or an unlucky cop with a free official-issue

Beretta or Smith & Wesson (none of us shoot Smiths anymore, do we?[1]), leave it at home.

The double-action semiautomatic was invented as a sop to citified grunts who were so dense they could not learn how to handle the big-bore single-action 1911 properly, and to gun-ignorant cops who could not stand to stare down at a cocked-and-locked pistol on their belt.

When I was a cop in plainclothes and wore a .45 Commander in an open-top holster inside my waistband, every single fellow cop who noticed would always point at it wide-eyed and ask me the same question: "Do you know that thing is cocked?" To which I would always answer, "Damn right I know it's cocked, and I know there's a gaping hollowpoint warming up in the chamber too."

The fact is, double-action autos are unnecessary handicaps in training (many instructors simply won't allow them), losing handicaps in competition, and potentially deadly handicaps on the street. Better to leave them to peacekeeping troops who are forced to carry their guns empty to intimidate people who don't know any better, to undertrained police forces like those in New York City and Washington, D.C. who routinely shoot to slide-lock without even scaring a bad guy, and to overmothered street-gang members who mow down innocent bystanders a block away every time they attempt a targeted drive-by (we really should teach those fatherless little bastards some marksmanship so they can kill each other off without disrupting entire neighborhoods).

Inelegant as double-action autos are, there have been even more overwrought attempts to avoid the manly rigors of basic training. An experienced cop showed up at a T.F.T.T. class once with a squeeze-cocking Heckler & Koch P7. The cop was proud of his very expensive and well made gun, and Max let him go through some simple draw-shoot-reholster exercises with the group. After a tedious hour of fumbling, mental confusion, and general embarrassment, the cop locked his outrageously complicated P7 in his car and borrowed a well-used Springfield Armory .45 from Max. We saw the cop often after that, but we never saw his P7 again. Actually, I've never seen another P7 anywhere since.

Glock's great leap forward in design and functionality was achieved by shunning the confounding and obsolete Waltheresque double-action mechanism and ridiculous gadgetry like the H&K squeeze-cocker and returning to and generally enhancing the fundamental principles of the 1911—simplicity, trigger control, and balance.

If you don't have a 1911, buy one. Learn to shoot it under professional (Marine) supervision. Once you've got it down, take your Glock to school and on to competition matches. And make sure it's the Glock you carry every day, not one you bought special because you thought it might give you some competitive advantage over your friends.

Every Glock I own I have shot in at least a handful of both IPSC and IDPA matches. And, no, I never quite equaled the scores I could have achieved with any of my competition-tuned 1911s. That was not the point.

The tiny .40-caliber G27's short sight radius slows down longer-range shooting for accuracy. The 10mm G29's stout recoil lengthens time between shots (and will give you a sore hand by the end of the day). The little .45-caliber G36's even stouter recoil (I shoot hardball in competition) and limited magazine capacity consume

It is not possible to get too much good training, but it is possible to win too many cheap medals. Photo by the author.

time all over the place on long IPSC run-and-gun stages.

The 10mm G20 I set up for hunting with a red-dot sight, 20-round magazines, and extended barrel brought my scores way up, but I defy anyone of normal size to effectively conceal this big gun beneath a jacket in any kind of holster at all.

And let it be known for competition purposes that no Glock magazine, not even the latest steel-lined so-called "drop-free" variety, provides the quick and slick reloads you can take for granted in a single-stack 1911. Gaston Glock designed his magazines to stay in his pistols until they were deliberately removed, following accepted European military doctrine, and his later attempt to make them squirt out like 1911 magazines just to satisfy IPSC shooters was half-hearted.

Shooting my Glocks in competition taught me to resign myself to shooting for a higher purpose, before God and everybody, a score which would have embarrassed me had I shot it with a big, highly tuned Government Model equipped with modifications worth the price of a new Japanese car. Once more, the score was not the point.

I learned the capabilities and limitations of each man-gun combination, a familiarity under pressure with the personalities of each individual pistol, a solid confidence in the reliability of my guns (I experienced not one malfunction of any kind, ever, shooting any Glock in the rushed and sometimes heavy-handed course of

The score is not the point.

competition), and the conviction in each case that my Glock and I had every capability required to end a gunfight in the proper manner. And that was the point.

The things you learn in modern shooting schools and practice in modern combat-oriented competition are important. You learn things like the proper two-handed grip—you grip a Glock just like you grip a 1911, not like you grip a double-action auto with its contrary upside-down thumb safety/decocker/entertainment device. You learn the strongest stance—the Isosceles may be the current rage among gamesmen, FBI agents-in-training, and females shooting .22s at tin cans, and the controversial Center Axis Relock may be this year's darling among those who reinvent the wheel for a living, but the Weaver or Modified Weaver is still the proper fighting stance whether you're operating a gun or a blade or a fist. You learn the strong-side draw and presentation and other tactical necessities of the Modern Technique such as the double-tap and safety drill and all kinds of other important things.

SPEED IS FINE BUT ACCURACY IS FINAL

A combat-oriented shooting school will even teach you a little about sight picture and sight alignment and breathing, but not nearly enough. You're supposed to have learned these classic fundamentals of marksmanship earlier, shooting NRA bull's-eye, but so many of the modern crop of action pistol shooters didn't, and it can be a pitiful sight to behold.

These upstart hotshots can nail a big target at 15 feet with a lightly recoiling handgun at blistering speed but couldn't shoot a hole in a silver dollar at 50 yards in a year of trying. They don't even understand why anyone would want to do such a thing. The possibility never occurs to them that they or theirs might someday be under fire from a man with a scope-sighted rifle. Or that

accuracy at 50 yards easily translates to accuracy at 25, 15, and 10. They would never imagine themselves in a situation where one of their hands was riddled with bullets and the only way to save their life was with one long shot with one weak hand. They've never heard or never believed the phrase, "Speed is fine but accuracy is final."

There are a few life-saving skills generally ignored by most, though not all, of today's handgun trainers and competition course designers. These include long-range shooting for accuracy, low-light shooting, and, if you're of like mind with me, draw and presentation from a shoulder holster. These are things you can practice on your own or, better yet, with a motivated partner or two.

One more thing you need to learn is how better to protect the lives of those around you in case a firefight erupts. You don't have to be yearning for the glamorous life of a Hollywood bodyguard to justify taking that VIP Protection course.

When drilling with a partner, inject a little competitive spirit into your sessions by using a timer. Concentrate on accuracy at long range, push yourself for speed at close range, train your finger to the rapid Glock trigger reset, focus on target identification under low-light conditions. The more you practice the more surprised you'll be at just how fast you can go while maintaining control.

If you're going to practice drawing from a shoulder holster, please take note that the entire 180-degree arc your muzzle covers each time you move your Glock from its in-holster backward-pointing position to the target in front of you must be back-stopped or clear for miles around. And remember that the importance of this practice is not so much speed but ingraining the doctrine that prevents you from covering your own weak arm during the sweeping draw. There just aren't many things more embarrassing than shooting yourself and living to tell about it.

HANDGUN COMPETITION DISCIPLINES AND ORGANIZATIONS

IPSC/USPSA: When Jeff Cooper and his buddies got together in Los Angeles back in the 1950s and did a little shooting together under the moniker Southwest Pistol League, an entirely new doctrine of the defensive handgun quickly evolved. It was called the Modern Technique of the Pistol, and it elevated the practice of combat shooting among civilians, military, and law enforcement to the startling levels of effectiveness we see today. Soon the organizers took over civilian competition and changed "combat shooting" to "practical shooting" in the name of political correctness. The International Practical Shooting Confederation and its U.S. counterpart, the United States Practical Shooting Association, were born. Soon after that the game-players took over and at that point should have changed the description from "practical shooting" to "impractical plinking." IPSC shooters win matches by running across open fields dumping magazine after magazine into the dirt. Nevertheless, competing in this fast-action sport can teach you a lot of things about you and your gun. Just remember that a little bit of IPSC goes a long way. E-mail: office@uspsa.org; Web site: www.uspsa.org.

IDPA: The more gamey IPSC became, the more serious shooters drifted away from it. In the mid-1990s, legendary 1911 shooter and pistolsmith Bill Wilson started up a new organization called the International Defensive Pistol Association in the hope of restoring a respect for sensible tactics to the combat shooting game. The effort has, in large part, proved effective, and IDPA is where you'll find real-world shooters competing today. It's not as much fun for the spectators to watch as IPSC (no race guns allowed), and you won't get off nearly as many rounds, but each round will count far more in your training regimen. E-mail: info@idpa.com; Web site: www.idpa.com.

GSSF: Glock realized early on that its mushrooming ranks of civilian Glock owners would have more fun with their guns and buy even more if they could enjoy the camaraderie of fellow "Glocksters" and compete now and then in low-key shooting matches designed not for brutal professional and semipro competition provided by the likes of IPSC but simply to familiarize themselves with the little black guns for which they had developed an abiding affection. Glock Shooting Sport Foundation matches are simple events—no drawing from holsters allowed and no tactics required—peopled by families with children, grandmothers, housewives and working women, men who would never pull the trigger on their home-protection Glock otherwise, and a few sandbagging master shooters providing free entertainment. The shoots are fun and relaxing, and almost nobody is there to win. In fact, prizes are awarded in so many categories it's almost a random draw that determines who takes something home as proof of his or her advancing skill. GSSF shoots, unlike the hard-core competition circuit events, are relatively few and far between but worth a visit on a lazy weekend afternoon. Web site: www.gssfonline.com.

NRA: The mother organization of all American shooters continues to offer a wide range of competition, relatively little of it cutting-edge but all of it worthwhile. As has been said before, NRA bull's-eye steadfastly defends the fundamentals of marksmanship even though electronic sights are now allowed for the aging competitors. NRA Action Pistol is an easier version of the IPSC discipline, Olympic shooters can hone their skills under the steady eyes of NRA instructors, and high-level police training is offered in submachine guns and other exotic and specialized weapons. I'm not going to list here the contact information for the various divisions of the NRA because, if you're a member, you get one of their monthly publications, which always contains those numbers. And if you're not an NRA member, you're not getting any help from me.

OTHER: There is no shortage of handgun shooting sports. Fun-oriented events like knocking down metallic silhouettes at long range can go a long way toward plugging the gaping hole unfilled by short-range combat shooting. Clearing a table of bowling pins (deceptively hard to kill) can materially increase your speed with heavy-recoiling pistols. Youth-oriented .22 events get the kids off to a good start. Check all your local gun clubs to see what's on their schedules.

FIREARMS TRAINING SCHOOLS

There's an ever-growing number of shooting schools all across the country, more than a hundred at last count. I'm sure that many of them are excellent. Some are surely not. I'm only going to mention the world-class schools with which I've had long personal experience or with which close shooting friends of mine have had long personal experience. These can be recommended without reservation.

GUNSITE ACADEMY: Jeff Cooper's school, the one that started it all, in Paulden, Arizona. Originally called The American Pistol Institute, Gunsite has graduated many of the instructors in the other first-rate shooting schools. Although it has gone through a couple of changes in ownership (one bad and one good), Cooper seems to be happy with the current ownership and has returned to personally teach a Master Series of classes at the pioneering school he founded. Web site: www.gunsite.net

TACTICAL FIREARMS TRAINING TEAM: Max Joseph's hard-core training group based in Southern California with facilities that include a 2,200-square-foot, 360-degree shooting house. But if you don't live in the

The hard-core Tactical Firearms Training Team (T.F.T.T.) was the first full-time firearms training academy on the West Coast and, in the author's opinion, is by far the best. Director Max Joseph, shown here, is a Marine who has been both student and instructor in the most advanced training offered by the U.S. Marine Corps, Army, and Navy. Photo by T.F.T.T.

People's Republic and don't even want to go there, Max has a "have gun will travel" policy that will take him and his professional crew anywhere in the country or the world. Max is the only man I know—or, frankly, ever heard of—who, after making a name for himself as a Recon Marine, reenlisted only on the condition that the Marine Corps put him through the Army's Ranger and Airborne schools. Max is an instructor's instructor and a shooter's shooter. Personally, I consider the black T.F.T.T. shirt Max issues if and when he's satisfied with your performance my single most valued badge of accomplishment. Absolutely first-rate, high-speed, and good to go. E-mail: director@tftt.com; Web site: www.tftt.com.

THUNDER RANCH: Ex-Gunsite Dean of Instruction Clint Smith's 2,400-acre state-of-the-art spread down in the hill country of Mountain Home, Texas. Facilities-rich environment and solid instruction. Web site: www.thunderranchinc.com.

•••

1   In the spring of 2000, Smith & Wesson made a deal with the devil. Bill Clinton extorted the great old American company (it was not well-known by shooters at that time that S&W was actually owned by a British

Top: Explosive entry and team training are not for the faint-hearted. Note Glock man Alan Roy in #2 position. Photo by T.F.T.T.

Middle: Firing with subgun speed, Alan Roy executes an extreme close-quarters drill. The IPSC-style target is even deader than it looks. Photo by T.F.T.T.

Bottom: IDPA competition emphasizes life-saving tactics that IPSC too often ignores. Photo by T.F.T.T.

conglomerate) and then-S&W president Ed Schultz into signing an agreement that fairly spat on the Second Amendment to the U.S. Constitution. Promoted by Clinton and his unholy legions in Congress and the media as "common sense gun safety," the infamous document actually went so far as to create an outside "oversight commission"—in plain English a new government bureaucracy made up of antigun local, state, and federal officials to supervise the gun manufacturer—to monitor and enforce the agreement as only government bureaucrats can. It was widely expected that other handgun manufacturers would be forced to sign the suicide pact as well. None

of them did. Glock said, "the company can make its business decisions independently without any interference from the government," thank you very much. Suffice it to say that a massive consumer boycott of Smith & Wesson ensued and sales quickly plummeted to half their previous levels. In the Spring of 2001, S&W was sold to an American company, Saf-T-Hammer Corp. in Scottsdale, Arizona. We shall see whether the new owners tell politicians what to do with that profane agreement and all the commemorative fountain pens used to sign it so that Smith & Wesson may once again be allowed into the civilized world of handgun shooters.

Glock 36: Exquisite Defense

4

The single-stack .45-caliber Glock 36 is dedicated to one thing and one thing only—saving your one and only butt. It is not a competition gun, though it wouldn't hurt to take one through a match for practice. It is not a hunting gun, though it's as good as any other .45 ACP for this purpose. It is not an offensive gun, unless your quarry is a single target at not much over 50 yards. Neither is the G36 the best choice as a home defense gun, as its magazine capacity is limited by its slim grip, and the streamlined frame does not allow the recent Glock feature of built-in rails that are particularly useful for attaching a tactical light.

But what might be unnecessary limitations on a gun bred to openly roam your castle like a Doberman become great strengths on a gun bred to live unobtrusively in the darkness beneath your jacket like a black mamba until it suddenly bursts forth to save your life.

The G36 is not a fat Glock with skinny grips, as most gun magazine reviewers have allowed readers to infer. And it is not a chopped and channeled version, in the best hot rod tradition, of a big old .45. Nor is it, like its larger .45-caliber Glock siblings, the G21 and G30, a brawny 10mm given a less demanding job. The single-stack .45-caliber G36 is an all-new Glock, designed and built fresh from the ground up with an awe-inspiring focus on its ultimate defensive purpose.

The G36 is a true big-bore handgun, with all of the real and mythical fight-stopping advantages of the .45 ACP round, packaged in a compact polymer frame the size and weight of which, but a few years ago in the pre-Glock era,

31

would hardly have been up to handling a conservatively loaded 9mm.

Okay, .40 fans can argue that the .45-caliber G36 is only millimeters smaller in all critical dimensions than the .40-caliber G23 but holds half as many rounds (in the G23's preban configuration). And that is true. But, in concealed carry, millimeters count—especially girth, and the G36 is even thinner than the little G27 (which is exactly the same thickness as the G23). And if it takes more than six or seven rounds between reloads to defend yourself, somebody should have issued you an M16 when you got out of bed this morning. Finally, as good as the .40 is, it makes a noticeably smaller hole in a bad guy than a .45, before and after expansion, entry channel and exit wound alike.

IN THE BEGINNING, THERE WAS THE .45

Every cop who has worked narcotics has heard the true story of the kid whacked out on horse steroids who bit through his handcuffs. Now I'm not going to suggest that such a chemically created monster would chew up and spit out lesser-caliber bullets, but I can pretty much guarantee he would choke on a big .45 slug.

Put it this way—if your measure of the effectiveness of a defense round is the amount of time, detergent, and manpower required to clean

Glock 36 is a big-bore pistol that goes anywhere. Photo by the author.

up the mess on the wall behind your attacker after the argument is over, then you'll appreciate the superior charm of the .45. (If things just can't get gory enough for you, have your tailor let out your jackets to accommodate a big 10mm.)

Of course, those who imagine every confrontation turning into a running gun battle, IPSC style, will not be dissuaded from trying to carry an IPSC-style gun. We can only hope, for their own good, that if they should ever find themselves in a firefight they don't play by IPSC rules.

A carry gun must balance concealability with firepower; that is, length, height, thickness, and weight with caliber and capacity. Depending on how prepared you want to be (how much you value your life) and what method you choose to attach your life-saving device to your body, there's a Glock that's beautifully balanced to suit your needs. This is one of the facets of balance that makes the Glock so appealing to professionals and why so many shooters own (and often carry) more than one.

If you start with the premise that you'd rather carry a .45, and if you'd like that carry to be as painless as possible, then the G36 is your gun, for several cumulatively compelling reasons:

To repeat, *it's a .45.*

At less than 27 ounces fully loaded, it's about

In concealed carry, millimeters count.

the lightest .45 you could ever hope to carry.

Size-wise, Goldilocks would love it. Not a fraction of a fraction of an inch is wasted, but it fills your hand (your entire hand) with a secure grip because a .45 is not something you want to hold by three fingers if you can help it.

It's thin and shapely enough to fit snugly up against your body wherever on your body you want to snug it up against.

It's a delight to handle. You'll find yourself wanting to twirl it around on your trigger finger like movie cowboys twirl their single-action revolvers. Don't do that. It is not a single-action revolver . . .

It's a Glock. You won't be wondering if it's going to go off when you pull the trigger.

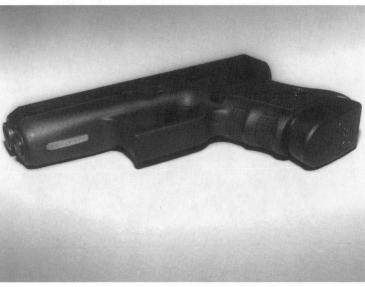

The .45 ACP Glock 36 is slimmer than any of Glock's 9mm and .40 models. Photo by the author.

AND THEN THERE WAS RECOIL

That's the carrying part. The shooting part is a different story. The G36's exceedingly friendly "carry personality" aside, when fed its intended diet of heavy defense loads, its felt recoil is downright fierce. It hurts your hand (but imagine what it feels like on the other end). Pulls even more willfully on the reins than the compact, but still much larger, 10mm G29. If you're the recoil-sensitive type, after you've run a few hundred rounds of ammo through it to stretch its legs and clear its throat, you may only want to bring it out on occasion to remind it (and

yourself) of that special occasion for which it was bred. Or you may want to feed it a steady diet of lightweight hyper-velocity low-recoiling frangibles like MagSafes, exotic and deadly loads perfectly suited to the G36. Or you might get to like the recoil for the same reason you might like to ride a spirited stallion instead of an easygoing gelding.

Recoil is not a factor in a carry gun unless it truly affects controllability, and that's not likely to happen to an experienced handgunner unless he's a weakling trying to fan the hammer of a .475 Linebaugh. The fact is, in a firefight, you probably won't feel any pain (right away) even if you get shot in the testicles, much less from a little slap on the palm of your hand from the cavalry riding to your rescue.

Handgunners who are afraid of a little recoil tend to fall into the "spray and pray" category of shooters. They don't just *like* high-capacity 9mms, they *rely* on them to make up for their own lack of experience, discipline, confidence, and responsibility. In case of panic, pull the trigger. Well, it doesn't work that way, and these people often get killed (which they deserve), as well as getting a lot of innocent bystanders killed (which *they* usually *don't* deserve). In fact, spray-and-prayers, especially big-city-law-enforcement spray-and-prayers, kill plenty of innocent

Recoil is not a factor in a carry gun.

bystanders every year all by themselves. Just read the papers.

The solution, of course, is training. And if you happen to have a friend who specifically suffers from the recoil-shy affliction, don't treat him like a baby. Don't suggest he revert back to a .22 and work his way up through .380s and .38s and 9mms before he tries to shoot a real gun. Take him to the range, plant a steel target at least 25 yards away from him up against a big dirt berm, put a double-action .44 Magnum in his hand, give him two or three 50-round boxes of full-power ammo, and leave him there for the day. He'll get over it.

THE MIND-SET OF THE SNIPER

A shooter who has the discipline and confidence to take responsibility for every trigger pull falls into the "one shot, one kill" category, and this is a far better place to be, whether you're a military sniper or a well-trained citizen prepared to defend yourself and other innocents from attack, whether you're a rifleman with a single opportunity to complete your 1,000-yard mission or a handgunner making your programmed kill three times over in the classic "Mozambique" manner of a double-tap to the

If you're going to tempt fate, better have one of these in your holster. Photo by the author.

chest and a safety shot to the head.

In fact, "one shot, one kill" is the only mind-set appropriate for anyone who carries a gun. It simply means that when you pull the trigger, you have every reason to believe you'll hit what you're aiming at. As in every other aspect of shooting, mind-set is what matters most.

As you may have surmised, the G36 is my current romance and constant companion on all professional and social occasions. It wears dazzling green and yellow Trijicons and, under nothing more than an open shirt, rides in a cutaway Galco Miami rig with a half-harness (I've found a local saddlemaker to amputate the offending safety strap under clinical conditions, as I haven't yet been able to persuade the factory to do it). When a jacket is called for, the G36 nestles in a Tauris shoulder rig, whose roomy fit, slick snap, and unobtrusive safety strap require no surgery. The two extra magazines, kept readily at hand to feed the curvaceous little Glock should it develop a sudden appetite, fit nicely on my belt. We have a very happy relationship.

My .40s, except for one well-placed hideout G27 and my lit-up G23 house gun, currently

If your measure of the effectiveness of a defense round is the amount of time, detergent, and manpower required to clean up the mess on the wall behind your attacker, then you'll appreciate the superior charm of the .45.

languish in the safe most of the days. My 10mms are usually content to spend most of their time at home as well, though there is one long-legged show-off G20 who, like an eager puppy, is always yearning to get out and accompany us for long walks in the deep woods.

Enhanced Glock 20: Lethal Offense

5

The 10mm is as powerful, well balanced, and practical a pistol cartridge as a mind like Jeff Cooper could imagine. It improves in every way on both the .45 ACP (first time that's been done in a hundred years) and the .357 Magnum.

The only problem, to relate it to a situation typical in another kind of industry, is that the software, if you can call a 10mm soft, has outdistanced most of the hardware. To date, the 10mm has wrecked every handgun it's been chambered in with the singular exception of the Glock.

Glock designed the G20 from concept through execution specifically to surpass the original FBI requirement for a 40,000-round endurance test using full-power 10mm ammunition. Other manufacturers going after the FBI contract—including Smith & Wesson, whose unloved 1076 was finally chosen by the Bureau—scrambled to adapt their old .45 frames to handle the later FBI specs for the reduced power 10mm "Lite" loading, which is no more than a .40 with a lot of wasted space. (By comparison, the original Norma 10mm load drives a 200-grain bullet at 1,200 fps, where the Federal 10mm FBI Lite load drives a 180-grain bullet at 975 fps.) You can accurately say that the Glock 20/29 is the *only* true 10mm pistol on the market, all others being nothing more than .45s stretched beyond the breaking point.

The big G20 is difficult for most people to carry discreetly concealed, but the compact G29 hides well for those accustomed to carrying a gun of substantial size. Personally, I would never venture past the city limits without one.

The 10mm G20 really comes into its own as a weapon of offense, for those occasions when you have time to set up and take the initiative—whether hunting, attacking a holed-up enemy, or pretending to do so in fast and furious competition.

Offense assumes certain tactical advantages, such as the element of surprise, superior firepower, and plenty of cover—soft cover if you're hunting, hard cover if the animal defending itself can be expected to shoot back, imaginary cover if you're just playing a game. In many ways, the offensive mind-set is easier to acquire and demands less training than the defensive mind-set, where it's more often muscle memory than marksmanship that saves your life.

While it is true that the best defense is a good offense, preemptive strikes are seldom condoned in courts of law that award all tactical advantages to criminal aggression. So your offensive weapon is likely to be employed openly in hunting fields or on competition courses, not covertly on dark streets against drug dealers and gangland killers where such action would do the most good. (Unless you're Charles Bronson who, today, would surely leave his unwieldy gas-operated Wildey in a kitchen drawer and take to the streets with a Glock 20.)

For the offensive rather than defensive handgunner, the 10mm cartridge on the full-size

The powerful and versatile 10mm Glock 20 is easily configured for any mission. Photo by Morgan W. Boatman.

Glock 20 platform is a union arranged in heaven by the guardian angels of Jeff Cooper and Gaston Glock, and there aren't a hell of a lot of things you can do to improve perfection.

There are, however, quite a few things you can do to make this gun your own.

Given its offensive nature and the correlative fact that size doesn't much matter, you can make it bigger to optimize its aggressive capabilities. You can give it a longer barrel, higher-capacity magazines, even an electronic sight. You can give it a lighter trigger pull for more contemplative shooting, and you can replace a few of its steel inner parts with exotic titanium if you so choose. And you can do all of this for about the same cost as a quality production-line hunting rifle with a scope, and less than half the cost of a customized competition 1911.

A LONGER BARREL

The standard slide-flush barrel of the G20 is 4.6 inches long. The Glock factory makes what it calls a hunting barrel for the G20, which is a full 6 inches in length. Several custom barrel-makers such as Jarvis and Bar-Sto also make extended tubes for the G20.

To date, the 10mm has wrecked every handgun it's been chambered in, with the singular exception of the Glock.

A longer barrel burns more powder, which means higher velocity, flatter trajectory, longer range, greater impact, cleaner kills. (See chronographed comparisons between G20 barrels in Chapter 10: The Great Glock Watermelon Shoot.) And that 1.4 inches of militant snout extending beyond the Glock's slide can be further customized with compensating cuts or threaded for a sound suppressor if you're so inclined.

That Glock is justified in calling its 6-inch, 10mm tube a hunting barrel can be attested to by the undamaged meat in my freezer and the hairy heads hanging on my wall.

BIGGER MAGAZINES

Before 1994, the standard magazine capacity for the G20 was 15 rounds. It still is, though Glock is now forced to produce dumbed-down, Clintonized 10-rounders solely for export to American citizens. New and used preban 15-round factory magazines are still available on the market (check *Gun List* or *Shotgun News*) at ever-increasing prices—you'll be lucky to pay less than $125 per copy for unused ones, which can quickly make your magazines more expensive than your gun.

Extended floorplates, or base pads, are readily available to augment the firepower of high-capacity magazines still further. It is not legal, nor in most cases is it physically possible, to add these floorplates to the willfully impaired 10-round magazines, but it's okay to use high-capacity preban mags in a post-ban gun. So go out and pay whatever is necessary to stock up on the magazines

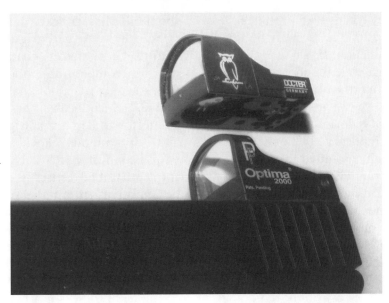

Optima red-dot sight is practically weightless and has a history of durability mounted directly on the G20's fast-stepping slide. New DOCTERsight from Germany has same features, slightly heavier construction. Photo by the author.

God and Gaston intended for you to use in your G20.

One of my personal favorites is the sturdy +5 floorplate from Grams Engineering, which includes a heavy-duty spring and well-designed follower. The last round is difficult to load into the magazine and I don't force it, figuring that 19+1 is 20, which is a nice round number and easy to keep track of when you're counting your shots as most instructors say you should. (Lots of luck counting your shots in a serious social engagement.)

With a 20-rounder in your magazine well and a couple more on your belt, you're not likely to run out of ammo in the hunting field or anywhere else.

BRIGHTER SIGHTS

While iron sights with tritium inserts are *de rigueur* on defensive Glocks, there's no reason why the big offensive Glocks shouldn't take full advantage of the latest, and often amazing, advances in electronic sighting equipment. One of the smallest and lightest of these is the Optima 2000 Pro Point illuminated red-dot from Tasco. This is the sight Glock installs at the factory on its Special Operations Command (SOCOM) qualified G21s.

Don't let the fact that the Optima is made in the U.K. dissuade you. While the Brits are no longer allowed to shoot anything, they're still allowed (as of this writing) to see the things they would have shot if they could. Like all things electronic, the Optima 2000 has steadily declined in price since its introduction. If you shop around, you can now get one for about half its suggested retail price plus the nominal cost of a Glock mount.

The polymer alloy Optima with its polymer optics is practically weightless at 1/2 ounce and has a history of durability mounted in the rear sight dovetail directly on the fast-stepping 10mm slide. There is no on/off switch—the unit is on all the time, except when you tuck it into your safe and slip the cover over it, which puts it to sleep—and the tiny Lithium battery still lasts for years. The Optima comes with your choice of a 3.5 minute-of-angle (MOA) or a 7 MOA dot size, which means that the very bright red dot appears to be either 3.5 or 7.0 inches in diameter on a target a hundred yards away. The 3.5 MOA dot is the better long-range and all-around solution, but the 7.0 MOA is excellent for extremely close and fast work.

A virtually identical red-dot sight has now been introduced from Germany. The ruggedly built DOCTERsight is about the same size and has all of the features of the Optima, differing only in that it is made of aluminum alloy and stainless steel with glass optics, so it weighs 1/2 ounce more. I have both the Optima and the DOCTERsight installed on two of my Glocks and can report that they both work exceedingly well.

If you're at that age when your eyes need all the help they can get, either of these excellent red-dot sights will give new clarity to your fuzzy sight picture and new life to your shooting.

BEGINNING EXPERIMENTATIONS WITH THE GLOCK TRIGGER

We've all been taught that an offensive gun should not have a heavy defensive trigger but rather a light "target" trigger, for obvious reasons. Glock makes such a trigger but offers it only on "competition" models. The standard Glock trigger has a nominal weight of 5.5 pounds, which means it has a 5.5-pound connector and an actual trigger pull weight more like 7 or 8 pounds. Glock's competition 3.5-pound connector yields an actual pull weight of about what it advertises its standard trigger to be. It also makes even heavier trigger mechanisms according to specs from liability-crazed police departments; it calls these "New York" triggers (but don't be tempted to give these triggers credit for the headline-making marksmanship of the NYPD).

None of these is nearly light enough for an experienced 1911 shooter, but there's not a hell of a lot you can do about it. Master gunsmiths can't help you. Glock innards are not designed to be fiddled with. Years ago, when I was a beginning Glock shooter, I figured the path to success was replacing parts, and continuing to replace them, mixing and matching connectors and springs and things and hoping to get lucky and stumble onto something close to that to which I was accustomed.

The G20 was the platform for all of my experimentations with the Glock trigger. My explorations began here and, given the preparatory attitude I've just expressed, took me to some quite unexpected places. The long journey ends in Chapter 14: The Enigmatic Glock Trigger, and you may be surprised at the conclusions that await you there.

I currently have a 3.5-pound connector installed in my G20. It's a third-party stainless steel unit with the so-called "BattleClad" finish from Glockworks in Old Saybrook, Connecticut. Whether or not it's an improvement over the standard is a subjective judgment we'll discuss later.

If you want to take your Glock apart and play with it, there are subtle things you can do.

TITANIUM AND STAINLESS STEEL

The part of a Glock that gets the most strenuous exercise, especially in a 10mm, is the recoil guide rod. When the polymer disc that mates to the underside of the barrel finally chipped on my factory guide rod, I transplanted a Glockworks stainless steel unit even though the gun continued to function fine with the chipped plastic. For no reason other than experimentation, I've replaced guide rods in some other of my Glocks with stainless and titanium units from Glockworks and Lightning Strike with good results.

If you want to take your Glock apart and play with it, there are subtle things you can do. For instance, you can decrease lock time a few milliseconds by replacing the striker, or firing pin, with one made out of titanium. I did this and more, replacing the striker and the safety plunger and even the trigger mechanism itself with titanium and aircraft aluminum parts made by Lightning Strike Products of Buford, Georgia, and

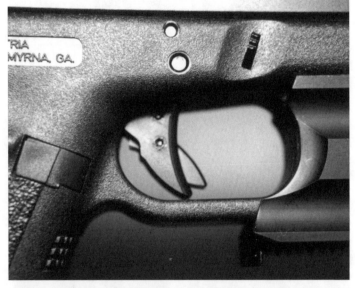

Top: Lightning Strike aircraft-aluminum trigger has shorter pull, smoother surfaces. Note the Las/Tac also attached. Photo by the author.

Above: Glock's integral rails accommodate a variety of accessories such as Laser Devices' Las/Tac laser sighting system. Also note the extended factory barrel and Glockworks stainless steel recoil guide rod. Photo by the author.

Cominolli Quality Custom Handguns of Syracuse, New York. Results have been satisfactory, but don't expect any miracles. You'll find a more complete discussion of these exotic parts in "The Enigmatic Glock Trigger" (Chapter 14).

ACCESSORIES ON RAILS

The only visible enhancement ever made by the Glock factory to the original design was modifying the grip specifications ever so slightly (this was first done when the G26/27 was introduced) so that all Glocks produced after that, except the thinner single-stack G36, now feel virtually the same in your hands no matter what the paper specs tell you. It was a good move. As if by magic, even the big G20 and G21 now fit your hands like pistols instead of two-by-fours.

At the same time (on all but the subcompacts) Glock molded rails into the underside of the receiver to accept accessories, including laser sighting units such as the built-like-a-tank Las/Tac from Laser Devices and powerful white lights such as the ultralight M-3 Tactical Illuminator from Insight Technology. An auxiliary laser used in conjunction with a red-dot leads to some interesting possibilities we'll discuss later, and a rail-mounted light may render the Harries and other flashlight-holding techniques obsolete, though it does not render the importance of a separate flashlight obsolete, as we'll also discuss later.

Day and night big and small game hunting package. Photo by the author.

And the red-dot and/or laser is state-of-the-art for guiding your hot 10mm missile into the small brain of a cold-blooded alligator.

You can add a recoil compensator (or, far better, buy a factory compensated G20C) and use ammo down-loaded to the .40 range and still make the major-caliber category in IPSC Open competition. The gun is versatile enough to configure precisely for just about any mission-specific requirement you might imagine.

A GAME GUN IN MORE WAYS THAN ONE

As a hunting gun, the G20 so equipped is quite capable of dropping a trophy mule deer in his tracks at 100 yards and more, coyotes and other varmints out as far as you can see them. If there's a better gun for close-up fast-action wild boar I don't know what it is. And you can let the pack mules keep that big chunk of .44 to themselves when you go promenading around in bear country.

Ted Nugent recently took his G20 to South Africa and came back with a 250-pound warthog, nailed with one round of Cor Bon 135-gr. JHP at 106 paces (the freedom-fighting rock-and-roller has long legs).

With the blinding white M-3 light attached, you've got a great 'coon gun, not to mention bitter medicine for other denizens of the night.

Bells and whistles notwithstanding, the G20 is still a user-friendly Glock, as easy and efficient in operation as any other. You will, however, require a little familiarization, as this is the biggest Glock you'll ever handle and the fancy sighting equipment can take a little getting used to.

As a jazz musician/combat shooter once told me, "Friend, whether it's a Selmer tenor sax or a 10mm Glock you've got in your hands, you gotta know how to wail on that thing."

So here you have what the gun-ignorant would call an "assault pistol," lacking only selective fire capability, a weakness that is easily, though not legally, overcome.

•••

Ted Nugent recently took his G20 to South Africa and came back with a 250-pound warthog, nailed with one round of Cor Bon 135-gr. JHP at 106 paces.

SOURCES

Lightning Strike Products, Inc.
4445 W-1 Commerce Drive
Buford, GA 30518
www.lspi.com
(Titanium, stainless steel, and aircraft
aluminum strikers, safety plungers, triggers,
guide rods, and other parts and accessories.
*Note: Lightning Strike has issued a recall on
reduced-travel triggers purchased between
January 2001 and September 2001. Check Web
site for more information.*)

Cominolli Quality Custom Handguns
624 Cherry Road
Syracuse, NY 13219
www.cominolli.com
(Glock competition triggers, tungsten guide
rods, manual safety conversions.)

Laser Devices, Inc.
2 Harris Court, A-4
Monterey, CA 93940
www.laserdevices.com
(Las-Tac laser and infrared aiming devices,
tactical flashlight systems, and laser-based
small arms training simulators.)

Insight Technology Incorporated
3 Technology Drive
Londonderry, NH 03053
www.insightlights.com
(M-3 white light Tactical Illuminator and
LAM white light & laser aiming module.)

Grams Engineering
2435 Norse Avenue
Costa Mesa, CA 92627
www.gramseng.com
(Extended base pads and other competition
parts.)

Tasco Sales, Inc.
2889 Commerce Parkway
Miramar, FL 33025
www.tascosales.com
(Optima 2000 red-dot sight distributor.
Product made in U.K.)

Eldorado Cartridge Corporation
12801 U.S. Highway 95 South
Boulder City, NV 89005
www.pmcammo.com/doctersight/
(DOCTERsight red-dot sight distributor.
Product made in Germany.)

Glockworks
Gunworks International, LLC
4 Center Road
Old Saybrook, CT 06475
www.glockworks.com
(Parts and accessories.)

Full-Auto Glock 18: Queen of Rock & Roll

6

If you ever get your hands on a select-fire Glock 18 you can kiss your coerced virginity goodbye. You'll understand why the Puritans among us have conspired to make such lascivious merrymaking illegal, and you'll curse them for it. Even if you have a torrid past filled with automatic weapons, you'll find there's nothing that quite measures up to a 22-ounce rock-and-roller with a 4.5-inch barrel.

WHY YOU NEED ONE

Prurient gratification aside, there are completely practical reasons competent civilians should have full and unimpeded access to submachine guns and machine pistols, one of which resides in the clear warning from the nation's founders that American citizens should always be as well-armed as the country's military and police forces.

If SWAT units need subguns to subdue criminals, if the Secret Service needs machine pistols to protect public servants, if the military needs select-fire assault rifles to preserve freedom, then American citizens defending their lives, their homes, and their loved ones need the same capabilities for all the same reasons. The premise has worked very well in Switzerland, pre-communist South Africa, and many other places around the world, including the United States until we lurched precipitously to the left in the 1930s.

When I was a little kid in Texas, I had a well-used High Standard .22 pistol that was my favorite jackrabbit gun. One

Reverse-engineering a Glock 18 produced this fire-breathing select-fire Glock 26. Photo by Eric Lorenzo Lim.

day, to my initial shock, the little semiauto started doubling. Within a week, as the worn sear went quickly after that, I owned one of the world's only fully automatic jackrabbit assault pistols. Every pull of the trigger sent a magazine-full of .22LR pills downrange. I had never had such fun before nor bagged as many jackrabbits (though their undamaged meat content trended downward). Unfortunately, the distinctive sound of automatic weapons fire coming from the woods behind our house eventually attracted the attention of my father, and he sent the gun in for repair. The memory of those most pleasant weeks rocking and rolling with a herd of jackrabbits in the backyard of my childhood came back in a flash with the first long burst I fired from the Glock 18.

It goes without saying that if you have a varmint in your sights, beast or man, a three-round burst is pretty much guaranteed to print a tighter group and therefore do more damage than a manual triple-tap. I'll be the first to admit

that this is territory where the 9mm reigns supreme. There are, indeed, times when a hornets' nest of 9mm slugs can be more effective than a single well-aimed .45 or 10mm bullet.

The muzzle rise of an uncompensated 9mm G18 (Glock makes a compensated model as well) in full-auto mode is quite controllable as long as you take a strong Weaver stance, lean into it a little, and hold the gun more toward the centerline of your body like you do a shoulder-stocked subgun. What makes this little spitfire fight back is its high cyclic rate of 1,200 rounds per minute—that's 20 rounds downrange every *second*. It took me the better part of an afternoon to develop a consistent feel for controlled bursts of three to five rounds. With its 17-round standard magazines or even the extended 33-rounders, you're not going to be spending much time shooting between reloads.

This kind of capability could easily promote the spray-and-pray technique beyond the limits of the imagination. You just have to remember that

Compensated Glock 18C requires plenty of ammo to feed its insatiable 1,200 rounds-per-minute cyclic rate. Photo by Glock.

what you're holding in your hands is a gun, not a garden hose, and focus accordingly. Nevertheless, there are times when you can get the job done better with a gun that goes *Zip* instead of *Bang*.

The selector lever on the G18 is right up there at the rear of the slide, so your thumb finds it on the low-bore-axis Glock almost as naturally as it finds the frame-mounted safety on a 1911. You can go from semiauto to full-auto and back again in an instant, a feature that largely makes up for the G18's extremely high rate of fire.

In the bodyguarding business in particular, the Glock 18 is the only 9mm worth carrying. And, on many assignments, it is definitely worth carrying indeed. The trouble is, unless you're a government employee, you can't.

WHY YOU CAN'T HAVE ONE

Even when Franklin Roosevelt signed the National Firearms Act of 1934, he knew it was unconstitutional to outlaw machine guns for civilian use. Besides, by that time western ranchers had grown attached to their .45-caliber Thompsons for pest reduction. So, in the first national exercise of stealth gun control, America's socialist-on-wheels levied a $200 tax on every transfer and required registration of all automatic weapons, sawed-off shotguns, short-barreled rifles, and "silencers," effectively shutting down the market in some extremely useful weapons. Sawed-off shotguns and short-barreled rifles are great to carry in the hunting field and, in Europe

There are times when you can get the job done better with a gun that goes *Zip* instead of *Bang*.

today, if you don't use a "silencer" on your hunting rifle you're considered a rude lout. (See the "Silent Glocks" chapter.)

By the time Ronald Reagan signed the oddly named Firearms Owners' Protection Act in 1986—the year the Glock 17 was introduced to America and a year before the Glock 18 was manufactured—respect for the U.S. Constitution had eroded even further. With that single signature, ownership of machine guns manufactured after that date was prohibited to civilians, period, thus slamming the door to the future. Machine guns manufactured prior to 1986 could still be owned subject to NFA rules, regulations, and taxes as before, providing that state laws did not specifically prohibit machine gun ownership, which several of them did. But not a single Glock 18 was manufactured before that unhappy deadline.

As an added insult, Bill Clinton's Crime Bill of 1994 outlawed newly manufactured magazines with a capacity of more than 10 rounds, which is just enough fuel to operate the already illegal G18 for a scant half-second.

We Americans seem uncharacteristically willing to give up hard-won and Constitutionally guaranteed freedoms for any dishonest politician's promise of a little crime control. But what kind of crime control? With more than 250,000 machine guns currently registered, half owned by civilians and half by police departments, there has been exactly one instance since 1934 when a legally owned machine gun was used in a crime, and that was a murder committed by a police officer.

Despite a plague of onerous requirements for federal registration, police approval, state approval, special taxes, waiting periods, and background checks already in place, and despite the perfect record of civilian machine gun ownership going on 70 years, in 1986 ownership of newly manufactured automatic weapons was prohibited to civilians forever.

That is not crime control. That is people control.

Our nation totters on the brink of tyranny when it allows only government-trained bodyguards hired to protect power-hungry politicians from angry constituents to use the most effective tools for the job, denying "ordinary" citizens the same ability to protect their own "ordinary" lives.

If your government would allow you to buy a G18, it would cost you no more than a G17 or any other Glock. The Glock pistol is already built to take the order-of-magnitude greater stress of fully automatic fire. And the select-fire mechanism is exceedingly simple, as one would expect from Glock.

I know a shooter in the Philippines who had his local gunsmith reverse-engineer the G18 and convert all his other Glocks to select-fire, including his G26, G17C, G19, and G21. How'd you like to go for a moonlight stroll through a gang-infested neighborhood with a full-auto G27 and a couple of spare 30-round magazines waiting patiently beneath your dinner jacket?

A European company is now marketing a small part that replaces the cover plate at the rear of the Glock slide, instantly converting the pistol to select-fire. It has a built-in selector switch, is interchangeable between all Glock

Our nation totters on the brink of tyranny when it allows only government-trained bodyguards hired to protect power-hungry politicians to use the most effective tools for the job, denying "ordinary" citizens the same ability to protect their own "ordinary" lives.

models and calibers, and attaches in about a minute. It sells for less than $300 and is already one of the most popular Glock accessories in Latin America. Too bad you can't pick one up at your local Banana Republic.

Whether you rock and roll when you get the chance or not, it's nice to know there's no limit to the uninhibited passion that lurks just waiting to be set free way down in your black pistol's soul.

The Man Who Knew Nothing About Guns

7

Gaston Glock is an unlikely figure to have inherited the mantle of John Browning. The little town of Deutsch-Wagram, Austria, home of the Glock family, is a suburb of Vienna, arguably the most elegant and gracious city in the world and unquestionably one of the principal ancient breeding grounds of Western Civilization. It is a world away from the wilds of Utah. Unlike Browning and most other giants of firearms design, Gaston Glock did not grow up with a gun in his hand.

During the 1950s, the talented Mr. Glock was an up-and-coming engineer and industrial plant manager. In 1963, he founded his own company, Glock Ges. M.b.H., to manufacture doorknobs and hinges, finally developing a line of military field equipment and police products such as knives, entrenching tools, training and fragmentation hand grenades, and nondisintegrating machine gun belts. Glock soon distinguished himself as an expert in working with and inventing new formulas for the space-age material called polymer.

In 1982, with no firearms manufacturing experience other than a stint at Steyr, Glock's entrepreneurial spirit got the better of him and he decided to go up against the mighty establishment of the European arms industry in competition for a new contract with the Republic of Austria's Ministry of Defense. The Austrian army needed a new semiautomatic 9mm combat pistol to replace its aging Walther P-38s, and the long-shot opportunity for Glock's young and ambitious company was as irresistible as it was unlikely.

The organizational and management genius that had already made Gaston Glock remarkably successful in a highly competitive business was once again called upon to solve what appeared from the outside to be an insurmountable challenge. Glock assembled a small but intensively talented group of Europe's most deeply experienced handgun experts—bright lights from the military, police, and private sectors with creative imaginations to match Gaston Glock's own and bursting with new ideas about handgun design, manufacture, and tactical deployment. Under Gaston Glock's leadership and motivation, Team Glock went to work.

Three months later—*three months later*—the Glock 17 was born.

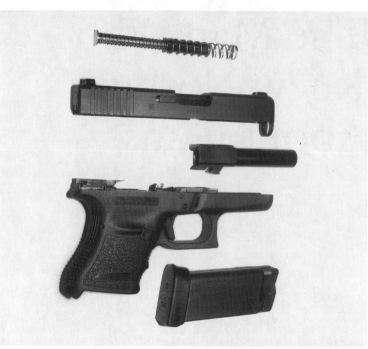

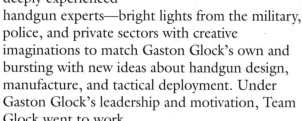

Simplicity and reliability are hallmarks of the unique Glock design. Photo by the author.

A PISTOL LIKE NO OTHER

The radical new pistol combined a receiver using Gaston Glock's patented Polymer 2 material, a steel slide machined from one solid rolled bar, and a revolutionary new "Safe Action" trigger mechanism. And the list of engineering breakthroughs and refinements that set the new Glock 17 apart from all other pistols went on from there, including:

- Polymer 2 receiver for strength, light weight, recoil absorption, and corrosion-resistance. (Polymer 2 is stronger than steel and 86 percent lighter. It is impact-resistant and virtually weatherproof, withstanding temperature variations between -49 and 392°F.)

- Carbon-steel slide CNC-machined from one solid rolled bar for maximum strength and integrity.

- "Safe Action" trigger mechanism for simplicity and reliability of operation. (Glock's "Safe Action" is actually the perfection of a system first explored in 1907 on the pioneering Austrian Roth-Steyr pistol. The unique "Safe Action" is called "Single-Action-Only" by some and "Double-Action-Only" by the BATF.)

- Fast 1/8-inch trigger reset for multiple high-speed follow-up shots.

- Multiple automatic safeties with no extraneous controls.

- "Cocks" and "uncocks" automatically with movement of the trigger, requiring no extraneous controls.

- Only 33 to 36 parts or components (depending on model and whether you count the sights or not) for operational reliability, lighter weight, simplicity of operation, and maintenance.

- Can be fieldstripped in seconds, with no tools, for thorough cleaning and inspection. Can be disassembled down to fundamental components in the field with nothing more than a simple pin punch.

- Component interchangeability between pistols for field maintenance, efficiency, and versatility.

- Self-lubricating, Teflon-nickel-coated lockwork for minimum maintenance. Chrome steel frame rails.
- No more than three drops of oil are recommended by the factory for thorough lubrication of the entire pistol.
- Proprietary Tenifer-finished slide, inside and outside of barrel. (Tenifer is actually a penetrating heat treatment that gives steel a skin hardness of 69 Rockwell Cone [RC], just a point or two less than industrial diamonds. Tenifer-treated steel is substantially harder and more rust-resistant and salt-water-corrosion resistant [99%] than stainless steel, Teflon, or hard chrome.) On top of the Tenifer treatment, Glock slides and barrels are coated with nonreflective black phosphate.
- Hammer-forged rifling vs. conventional square-cut rifling produces stronger, more durable barrels with greater wall thickness and molecular density in the polygonal rifling. Glock barrels are independently proofed at Vienna Proof House at twice the standard pressures over 25 repetitions.
- Barrels manufactured with slightly oversize chambers for an extra measure of feeding reliability and slightly undersize bores for tighter gas seals, increased velocity and stability.

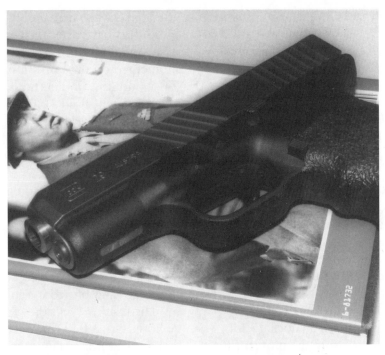

Glocks are built to go to war. Photo by the author.

- Barrel, chamber, and lugs machined from one solid steel block requiring no conventional swinging links, barrel bushings, or attachment to the receiver for more positive barrel lock-up, enhanced accuracy potential, easier take-down, and greater reliability.
- Naturally pointing ergonomic grip angle.
- Low bore axis to reduce muzzle flip and felt recoil.
- Extremely quick cycling and superior action balance for fast and reliable tactical performance with a broad range of ammunition.
- Designed to accommodate ambidextrous and one-handed shooting techniques.
- Flawless technical service and customer support.

Within months of submission, stringent army testing had proved the Glock 17 clearly superior to all competition—including models submitted by Heckler & Koch, Sig-Sauer, Beretta, FN, and Steyr—and Glock's black polymer creation was chosen as the official service pistol of the Austrian army. The initial purchase of 30,000 guns was

Gaston Glock did not know that guns were ever supposed to fail. So he built them so they wouldn't.

delivered in short order thanks to the manufacturing efficiencies inherent in the Glock design, and handgun professionals all over the globe quickly got their hands on their first astonishing Glock pistol. The rest, as they say, is history.

CONTROVERSY, TORTURE, AND THE BEST REVENGE

Introduced to the American public in 1986, the Glock 17 was met with howls and yelps from the antigun crowd accusing the little black pistol of being so radical in its state-of-the-art design that it had already become the weapon of choice for sophisticated international terrorists. One of the first and loudest to clamor for banning all civilian ownership of Glocks was New York City Police Commissioner Benjamin Ward, who, it was later discovered, had carried a Glock 17 for his own personal protection from the moment he first got his hands on one.

Like the nonstop rifles of Mikhail Kalashnikov, Gaston Glock's handguns are designed to go to war anywhere in the world, enduring extreme rigors that quickly destroy arms intended for less demanding employment.

Glocks have been thrown off the roofs of six-story buildings onto concrete parking lots, submerged on the bottom of the Pacific Ocean for six months, fired a thousand rounds nonstop in 45 minutes, fired 10,000 rounds without cleaning or lubrication, fired underwater, subjected to the astronomical pressures of firing two bullets from the barrel at once, drawn from leather and Kydex holsters a million times, tossed out the windows of speeding cars onto pavement, run over and parked on by an armored Suburban, dropped out of a helicopter, dragged behind a truck down a gravel road for miles, lost in a drainage ditch for three years, hidden beneath a Dumpster for 7 1/2 years, soaked in corrosive chemicals, and buried in sand and snow and mud.

The results? Well, the guns sometimes had to be hosed off before they were recognizable, and there was occasional cosmetic damage. But the abused Glocks never failed to fire and fire continuously after their ordeals.

Gaston Glock did not know that guns were ever supposed to fail. So he built them so they wouldn't. All 2.5 million of them, so far.

A Glock in Every Holster

8

Until the government starts issuing Glocks to every citizen, as it should, you'll have to be responsible for filling your own holsters. Given Glock's extraordinarily complete line of pistols and the specialized appeal of many of them, let's hope you have plenty of holsters that need filling.

G17 *(9mm):* The original, named after Gaston Glock's 17th patent. The only gun in the history of the world to survive Alan Roy's 322,000-round (at last count) endurance test and Chuck Taylor's 168,000-round (at last count) torture test that has included deliberate exposure to man-killing extremes of heat and cold, burials in dirt, mud, sand, and snow, six months at the bottom of the ocean, and total immersion in fresh cow dung. Both of these G17s continue to chatter along as merrily and glitch-free as ever. And the Austrian Hirtenberger ammunition factory is still counting the rounds fired through its single Glock 17—348,210 rounds so far, and the only parts replaced have been two springs.

This gun is so good it converted a lot of .45-shooters to 9mm until Glock started making guns in more serious calibers. The G17 is the mother of all Glocks and still the international best-seller. *Yo, mama!*

The 9mm Glock 17 is the mother of all Glocks. All product photos in this chapter by Glock.

G17C *(9mm, compensated)*: When IPSC competitors got their hands on the G17, the first thing they did was drill holes in the top of the slide and the barrel to further reduce what little muzzle rise the 9mm produced. This is an excellent example of how far away from the real world competition can get.

In a defensive situation, where you can't always assume the perfect grip and stance, the hot gases and fiery particles blasted up out of the top of your gun from a recoil compensator are prone to lighting up your buzz cut, temporarily blinding you, setting your shirt on fire, or worse. It's very much like shooting yourself, directly or with a near miss, with everything that should be rapidly leaving your muzzle toward the target except the bullet itself.

In a house gun, not only do you risk losing your sight but, because compensated guns are much louder than uncompensated guns, you run a greater risk of losing your hearing as well.

Nevertheless, to serve the strange needs of game-players, a cottage industry in hybrid Glock compensators quickly arose, which Glock forthwith put out of business by offering even more efficient factory-cut compensated models of their own.

Today, almost every Glock model other than the subcompacts is available in a "C" (for compensated) configuration, effective only with high-pressure loads (compensators have little effect on the laid-back pressures of a .45) and recommended *only* on a dedicated IPSC Open competition gun or perhaps on a big 10mm you promise to use only for hunting in broad daylight.

G17L *(9mm, long-slide)*: The growing clan of Glock competition shooters thought they

The 9mm Glock 17L has a greater expanse of real estate between the front and rear sights than the G17.

needed a longer sighting radius, so Glock obliged them. The "L" (for long) has a 1.53-inch longer barrel than the standard G17 (and is that much longer overall) and has a 1.58-inch longer sighting radius. The trigger pull is supposed to be a pound lighter than the standard but you can't always count on it.

The G17L is too long to carry comfortably, but the greater expanse of real estate between the front and rear sights helps precise aiming a little bit.

G18 (*9mm, select fire, law enforcement only*): Queen of Rock & Roll, fully covered in its own chapter. If the LEO designation ever comes off, buy one. If you run a well-trained and disciplined police department, buy a lot of them.

No, the compensated model is *not* recommended, for all the reasons discussed under the G17C times 20. If you can't handle a full-auto

9mm pistol whose barrel and slide haven't been mauled by a machinist, get a shoulder weapon.

G19 (*9mm, compact*): While competition shooters were clamoring for a longer Glock, defensive shooters were clamoring for a shorter one, and Glock obliged them as well. By whittling away .47 inch from the barrel and slide and .44 inch from the grip and overall height of the G17, Glock came out with a pistol that is just about the ideal size for daily carry. Neither too big nor too little, but just right, the G19/22 handles like a service pistol and carries like a dream.

G20 (*10mm*): Glock was one of the first major manufacturers to recognize the potential of the 10mm cartridge and quickly developed the *only* pistol that could handle this powerful round and go on ticking. The G20 is covered in its own

The select-fire G18 (shown in compensated
version) is a bodyguard's best friend.

The compact 9mm Glock 19 is an ideal carry size.

The 10mm Glock 20 (shown in compensated version) is the most powerful of all Glocks.

chapter—"Lethal Offense"—with some suggestions for quick and easy modifications that make this big gun as versatile as it is potent.

G21 *(.45 ACP)*: Once the large-frame G20 was built, it was a relatively easy matter to chamber the same brawny frame for America's most perennially popular big-bore cartridge, the .45 ACP. Glock's methodology worked far better than going about things the other way around, which resulted in several manufacturers' pathetic attempts to accommodate the high-pressure 10mm in frames designed for low-pressure .45 loads.

Consequently, the G21 is overbuilt and

therefore pretty much a waste of strength. That is, unless you're one of those people who reject any cartridge measured in millimeters instead of inches, or you plan to feed your .45 a constant diet of the hottest +P loads you can get your hands on or cook up on your own. In the latter case, the big Glock 21 (or its compact sister, the G30) is your only choice.

G22 *(.40)*: Glock was quick to realize that the 9mm G17 frame was easily strong enough to chamber the new, more powerful .40 round with the most minimal of modifications, and Gaston Glock went forth and did so, thus creating the G22/23. Glocks were the world's first

Glock was one of the first major manufacturers to recognize the potential of the 10mm cartridge and quickly developed the *only* pistol that could handle this powerful round and go on ticking.

The .45 Glock 21 is a service-size big-bore pistol popular with police departments.

The .40 Glock 22 offers more stopping power than its same-size 9mm sibling, the G17.

The compact .40 Glock 23 is one of the best concealed-carry guns in the world. The compensated version shown is not recommended for defensive carry.

production pistols to chamber the .40, even before Smith & Wesson who, with Winchester, was in on the development of the cartridge that changed American police firearm standards virtually overnight and effectively retired the 9mm from the U.S. law enforcement scene.

The .40-caliber G22 is the exact same size, and within less than an ounce of the exact same weight, as the 9mm G17. In fact, every 9mm Glock model except the G18 is also available in .40—same size, same weight, and substantially more effective.

G23 *(.40, compact)*: The downsized G23 immediately followed the service-size G22. With the exact same dimensions as the compact 9mm G19, the G23 is one of the very best concealed-

carry guns ever made. It can be found in the holsters of knowledgeable civilians and plainclothes cops all over the country and, along with the G22, is the current issue weapon for the FBI.

During FBI evaluation, one of the Bureau's many torture tests called for lodging a bullet in the barrel of the Glock one inch forward of the chamber. A round of full-power service ammunition was then fired in the obstructed bore. Rather than blowing up the gun, as any reasonable shooter may have expected to happen, the fired round cleared both bullets from the barrel and the Glock just kept on shooting.

G24 *(.40, long-slide)*: The .40 version of the 9mm G17L, for competitors who want to shoot a major caliber.

Glocks were the first production pistols to chamber the .40.

The long-slide .40 Glock 24 (shown in compensated version) is intended primarily for competition.

G25 *(.380 ACP, European only)*: As far as Americans are concerned, this gun is of no earthly use whatsoever. It occupies exactly the same holster space as the .40-caliber G23 and is manufactured purely to satisfy odd laws in some European and Latin American countries that prohibit civilians from owning military/police-caliber weapons such the 9mm G19, and for people who live in places so remote they have never heard of the .40. Adequate only for threatening northern Italian (not Sicilian) criminals who swoon at the sight of a brandished .25. Not intended for actually shooting people. Not available in the United States because nobody would buy one.

Well, okay, since the .380 is a subsonic round and therefore "silenceable" (as is the puny 147-grain subsonic 9mm that has got a few cops killed over the years), the G25 equipped with a good sound suppressor could conceivably be an acceptable way to exterminate all those rabid squirrels in your backyard without arousing the neighbors, or for the occasional cushy assassination assignment that requires no more than emptying a quiet magazine into the back of somebody's head (just make sure their hands are tied first).

G26 *(9mm, subcompact)*: The debut of the G26/27 mini-Glocks marked another milestone in the march of Gaston Glock through the gun-carrying populations of the world. These are

The debut of the G26/27 mini-Glocks marked another milestone in the march of Gaston Glock through the gun-carrying populations of the world.

The 9mm Glock 26 can go anywhere a snub-nose .38 revolver can go.

almost pocket pistols, though considerably thicker than the little .25s and .32s that normally define that category, chambered in decidedly nonpocket calibers, and equipped with relatively high-capacity magazines right up to the legal limit. Nobody had ever done that before.

Mr. Glock continued whittling away at the G19/23 until he had shaved another .56 inch off the barrel and, most importantly, another .82 inch off the bottom of the frame. You can't get your little finger around the stubby grips of the G26/27, though solutions for that are available if you really want to neutralize the major benefit of the gun, and concealability in a horizontal shoulder holster is only marginally improved. But when a mini-Glock is stuffed on the inside or outside of your waistband or in your underwear or a pocket holster, the difference between it and all other Glocks is substantial. The G26/27 has replaced the previously ubiquitous S&W J-frame in ankle holsters and other small, dark places all over the country.

For ladies who don't mind a somewhat

snappy recoil and can't get behind a shoulder holster, the 9mm G26 is an ideal purse gun—in a pocket holster, please, not loose among the lipstick tubes and hairbrushes and whatever else might occupy that mysterious space at any given moment (not that I would recommend off-the-body carry to any but my worst enemies anyway).

If you're not a lady, go with the noticeably snappier .40-caliber G27.

G27 (*.40, subcompact*): You get one less round (9+1 instead of 10+1) and just over one ounce more weight with two loaded magazines vs. the G26. Definitely worth the trade-off.

The G27 is a big gun for little places. World's best for reliable defense from deep concealment. Should be sold by the dozen (at least by the six-pack), so you could have handfuls for tucking away in various places on your body, in your car, home, and office, and wherever else you might someday need a small tool for an urgent job.

G28 (*.380 ACP, subcompact, European*

Same size as the little G26, the .40 Glock 27 delivers considerably more punch.

The 10mm Glock 29 is a powerhouse in a relatively small package.

The compact .45 Glock 30 is a handier version of the big G21.

only): See G25. A G26/27-size version of same. Just as useless.

G29 *(10mm, compact)*: A G20 you can carry. Like its big sister, the compact G29 was designed to handle as many full-power 10mm loads as you're likely to pump through it in a lifetime. Three ounces lighter, an inch shorter in the grip, almost an inch shorter in the barrel, but still not a small gun. I find the G29 extremely well balanced and a delight to shoot, if just a touch bulky beneath a jacket and unnecessarily powerful to carry in the city. But when you get on the road out there among the masses of humanity armed with sharp-edged multi-ton vehicles and whatever may be skulking inside, or off the road among the always-dangerous marijuana farmers and grizzly bears, it's awfully hard to beat.

The G29 is also the perfect backup to a G20 you've set up for hunting dangerous game, or for hunting any kind of game in country where dangerous game exists, and that includes quail hunting on farmland that also serves as pasture for not-always-entirely-domesticated locomotive-size bulls.

G30 *(.45 ACP, compact)*: Like the full-size G21, a bit of a waste in a frame designed to handle the 10mm, especially for those of us who believe a pistol should always be operating at its maximum potential.

The G27 is a big gun for little places. World's best for reliable defense from deep concealment.

The .357SIG Glock 31 was one of the first platforms for the new bottleneck cartridge.

The compact .357SIG Glock 32 is making some headway in law enforcement circles.

G31 *(.357SIG)*: It's pretty clear that Sig-Sauer engineers have too much time on their hands, especially now that so much of their handgun market share has been consumed by Glock. The thought process of the developers of the new .357SIG cartridge, for which Glock models 31, 32, and 33 are chambered, must have gone something like this, only in Swiss-flavored German:

"Well, you know, Ed Sanow and Evan Marshall and all those police-shootings-record-keeping-ballistics guys keep saying the 125-grain .357 Magnum is still the king of one-shot stops, so why don't we come up with a semiauto cartridge we can call a .357 and cut in on a little of that glory?"

So they necked down a .40-caliber case and stuck a 9mm bullet in it. *Voila!* Introducing the revolutionary new retarded .40, I mean .357SIG.

The G31s, 32s, and 33s are nothing more than G22s, 23s, and 27s with .357SIG barrels dropped in so you can make smaller holes, albeit at higher velocities. As superfluous as this new hybrid bottleneck cartridge seems to be, it is showing the same inherent accuracy as its namesake, and interest has stirred within certain traditional police circles that still reminisce over their reluctantly abandoned Smith revolvers of days gone by.

The 125-grain loadings for .357SIG semiautomatics and .357 Magnum revolvers have identical ballistics on paper, but their performance in gelatin is not so identical. There is not enough data on the .357SIG's performance in flesh and blood for any real opinions to be rendered. The weight of the bullets and the velocities achieved are the same for both rounds, but the construction of the bullets is different because of the divergent requirements of self-loading and revolver bullet design. The .357

Magnum loading which set the standard everyone tries to emulate carries a 125-grain semijacketed hollowpoint bullet with a lot of lead on its shoulder. The .357SIG's 125-grain bullet is, of course, a fully jacketed hollowpoint.

The best description I've heard of the great bottleneck wonder comes from Fernando Coelho, President of Triton Cartridge Co., who told me, "The .357SIG is really a 9mm+P++."

That's not a bad thing. But it's still a 9mm.

G32 *(.357SIG, compact)*: See G31.

G33 *(.357SIG, subcompact)*: See G31 again.

G34 *(9mm, long-slide)*: The G34/35 pistols are ever so slightly shorter versions of the G17L/G24 long-slides. They are designed specifically for new competition rules. They fit in the right-size box. Enough said.

G35 *(.40, long-slide)*: See G34. There are, however, some police departments who are fond of these longer Glocks because of their extended sight radius.

G36 *(.45 ACP, compact, single-stack)*: Another milestone for Glock. Unlike the .45-caliber G21 and G30, which were originally designed for the 10mm, the G36 was designed from the ground up as a .45, and one meant for concealed carry every day of its interminable life. An elegant and irresistible handgun. Tied neck-and-neck—the winner determined by the most subtle of personal preferences—with the G23 as the world's best carry gun. As a man of the-bigger-the-hole-the-better-I-feel persuasion, my vote goes to the G36, at least this month. Covered in its own chapter, "Exquisite Defense."

They necked down a .40-caliber case and stuck a 9mm bullet in it. *Voila!* Introducing the revolutionary new retarded .40, I mean .357 SIG.

The subcompact .357SIG Glock 33 is an ideal backup for those who favor the new cartridge.

The long-slide 9mm Glock 34 is a popular minor-caliber competition gun.

The long-slide .40 Glock 35 makes major-caliber for competition and has also developed a limited police following.

The Rainbow Glocks (*practice and training*): Glock also makes brightly colored toy guns for cops to play with. Since these plastic playthings are designed specifically to violate every safe gun-handling rule in the book, many of us consider their deployment a "risky training scheme." Nevertheless, they are quite popular in law enforcement training programs.

The one with the bright red frame and magazine floorplate is a real "dummy." It has the same weight and balance as a G17 and allows the student to practice loading, unloading, trigger operation and dry firing, manual manipulation of the slide, fieldstripping, and disassembly. But the red Glock's firing pin is deactivated, the breech-face has no firing pin hole, and the barrel is a hole-less bar of solid steel. It's perfectly foolproof and safe under any and all conditions and therefore, in my opinion, is extremely limited in its ability to teach anybody anything about guns since it is not one.

The Glock with the bright blue frame and magazine floorplate is the G17T 9mmFX, which, according to Glock, is "designed to fire color marking ammo" (paintballs, or simunitions if you want to be prissy about it). Or it might be the G17T 7.8x21AC, which is "chambered for reusable compressed air cartridge casings" (air gun) and also spits out little paint pills or rubber bands or whatever "without chemical propellants" for use in "sensitive environmental conditions."

The trouble with the blue Glocks is that people not only point them at each other but they actually shoot each other with them. Your father, who invested a great deal of serious time teaching you the fundamentals of gun safety, would not approve.

In writing this, I was prepared to dismiss the Rainbow Glocks because of my belief that people, raw cop recruits included, do not learn how to handle and shoot firearms by playing with toys. In my own faraway childhood, my interest in gunlike objects that made nothing but noise lasted about three weeks before I demanded and got my first Daisy. A .22 quickly followed, and by

The single-stack .45 Glock 36 is one of the two best concealed-carry guns in the world.

the time I was 11 I had my first .45, a loose but reliable Argentine model, which I started carrying on a regular basis at about age 14.

My understandable contempt for grown men who play with toy guns was about ready to burst forth on these pages when an eminent police trainer talked me out of it—for a reason I found shocking to the extreme and utterly unbelievable until I had researched it on my own.

A SHOCKING TRUTH

This police lieutenant, himself a veteran of a lethal gunfight, told me that the biggest single problem a combat firearms instructor faces—the problem that has probably got more innocents killed than any other—is the utter inability of many, indeed most, shooters to pull the trigger on another human being.

In World War II, only 15 to 20 percent of American riflemen were able to deliberately kill an enemy soldier with aimed fire. This is according to extensive studies by Brigadier General S.L.A. Marshall. Similar studies going back as far as The War Between the States confirm the phenomenon. In Vietnam, American soldiers fired 55,000 rounds for every enemy soldier they killed. Military analysts conclude that if men are directly accountable for killing a fellow human being, 80 to 85 percent simply can't do it. Modern police departments face the same problem—two out of ten law enforcement

The biggest single problem a combat firearms instructor faces is the utter inability of many shooters to pull the trigger on another human being.

applicants actually admit they could not or would not shoot a violent assailant even to save another officer's life.

Civilian concealed carry classes rarely address this issue in any depth. As a result, there are many people carrying guns who will not use them. Thanks to the entertainment industry, they believe they have only to wave a gun around to bring about the total submission of a hardened criminal equipped with well-honed killer instincts. We wish them luck.

All violent criminals reading this take heart. You have less to fear from the dreaded armed citizen than you thought. The next time someone interferes with your job by pulling a gun on you, just walk over and take it away from him. Beat the spineless twit to death with it or use it to kill someone else. Thanks to widespread cowardice and lack of intensively focused training, the odds are clearly in your favor. Do you feel lucky, punk?

If a blue Glock loaded up with little rubber balls full of red paint helps teach people that shooting and killing another human being is simply the final step of the draw, then I for one am all for it. Though I must cling to my belief that you only really learn to shoot real people by shooting real guns you know will kill them when you pull the trigger, whether deliberately or otherwise.

Glock makes plenty of real guns. They're the black ones. And they're meant to be used.

A Holster for Every Glock

9

As much as you might like the idea, you can't walk around with your Glock in your hand all the time. What would people say? It's not a good idea to just shove it in your waistband with nothing to prevent it from sliding headlong down your pant leg at the most inopportune moment. No professional would recommend you drop it unprotected in your pocket where it might get all tangled up in your piano-wire garrote.

You need a holster. In fact, you need a whole box full of holsters, because finding the perfect gun/holster combination is like finding the perfect gun itself, which is like finding the perfect woman—they're all meant to be lifelong pursuits, never quite fulfilled. As in all journeys toward idealized destinations, getting there is all the fun.

LEATHER HOLSTERS

Holsters have come a long way from the rough-hewn leather purses of old. Today, turning out effective gun-carrying rigs is perhaps the most vibrant aspect of the ancient art of the saddlemaker. From workshops in English cottages to big factory operations in the American desert, accomplished leather craftsmen with traditional hand tools work alongside technicians running giant machines to produce precision-molded holsters with a fit and finish, modern features, and an overall level of quality impossible to achieve in earlier times.

Like boots, holsters come in plain and fancy varieties, from cowhide and horsehide to exotics like alligator, shark, sting ray, ostrich, lizard, and python.

You can get a well-designed holster to fit strong-side on your belt, inside your waistband, behind your back, in the cross-draw position, riding over your shoulder and under your arm at vertical or horizontal or transverse angles, on your ankle or your thigh, on your hip or in your pocket. Some are minimal affairs designed for sheer speed of draw, others have ingenious thumb snaps and straps and flaps for maximum security and protection.

And there are accessories. Holders for spare magazines, handcuffs, flashlights, and other equipment are available separately or integrated into complete holster systems. If you wear a holster on your belt, you need a proper gun belt to hold it in the intended position. One of the most common mistakes a novice makes, and the primary source of holster-wearing discomfort, is hanging a substantial holstered gun on a thin little designer belt. Most makers of holsters also manufacture quality belts, many of

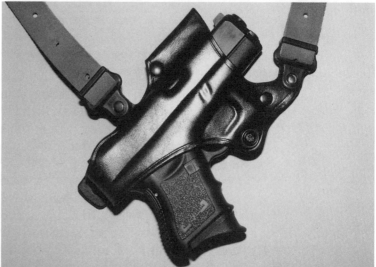

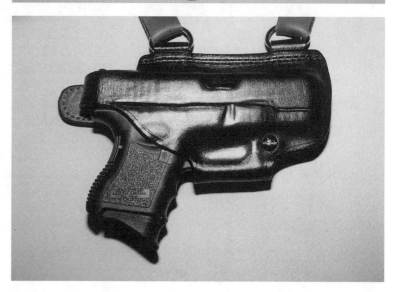

Top: With thumb strap amputated, the adjustable tension screw on this Galco shoulder holster provides ample security for all but the most strenuous of carry situations. Photo by the author.

Middle: Galco has recently reintroduced its original Jackass Rig, a true transverse shoulder holster for those who like to carry their gun at a more extreme angle. Photo by the author.

Bottom: Don Hume horizontal shoulder holster is an unusually rugged rig. Photo by the author.

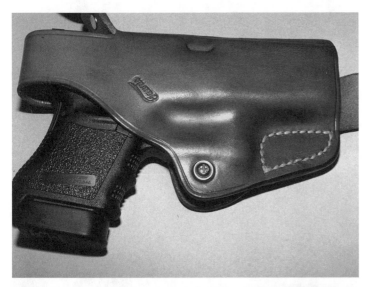

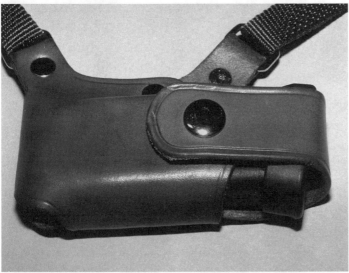

Top: Tauris horizontal shoulder holster has a superior snap system on the safety strap and is fitted more generously to the gun for rapid access. This holster doesn't even require any breaking-in period. Photo by the author.

Above: Offside single magazine carrier for the Tauris shoulder system is as compact, fast and glitch-free as the gun holster. It probably helps that Tauris owner Mike Taurisano is a cop. Photo by the author.

which can pass as dress belts, that are strong and rigid enough to prevent your gun from sagging as well as your pants.

After centuries of refinement, leather holsters have reached the peak of their development, and they are impressive indeed. But gun-carrying technology is by no means hidebound. An entirely new class of holsters has come on the scene over the last few years, following very closely in the footsteps of Glock pistols, and has now reached its own critical mass.

KYDEX HOLSTERS

Kydex is a term I'm using generically to describe various formulations of a space-age plastics material combining PVC and acrylic. It is easily thermo-formed from one-piece sheets and keeps its shape for life. It is extremely light in weight, thin but strong and durable, impact-resistant, abrasion-resistant, virtually impervious to chemicals and solvents, stable well beyond the parameters of human survival, and practically maintenance-free.

Because a Kydex holster can be precisely molded to fit the gun for which it is intended and because it has a rigid, permanent memory of that shape, these holsters provide a high level of inherent security along with very rapid deployment. It's extremely difficult to shake your gun out of a well-designed Kydex holster but extremely easy and fast to snatch it out in the course of a draw.

Drawing from a Kydex holster produces a distinctive "snap" sound, which causes some uneasiness in people who like a very stealthy draw, but leather holsters are not all that quiet either. In a defensive situation, it's a moot point in any case.

The custom manufacture of Kydex holsters began as a cottage industry because the material is easy to work by hand. But the booming popularity of these highly efficient and relatively low-cost products has seen many of the small manufacturers grow into substantial business enterprises and most of the established makers of leather holsters develop leather/Kydex hybrids as well as full Kydex lines of their own.

For pure sex appeal, it might comfort you to know that Kydex is also used to make the interiors of jet fighter cockpits. Primarily because of its negligible weight and slim dimensions, Kydex is rapidly becoming recognized as an ideal mate to the polymer frames of Glock pistols.

THE TACTICAL IMPERATIVE

Given the satisfying state of holster development today, routinely carrying one, two, three, or four guns is a practical proposition. But practical is not the same as tactical, and it's the tactical carrying of your gun or guns that can save your life.

To begin with, you need *one primary gun* and *one consistent carrying method* you will revert to under stress. Choose your system carefully and train with it. Make sure you can shoot not only with two hands but with both your strong and weak hands separately. And make sure that your draw doctrine precludes covering your own body with the muzzle of your gun and that the draw can be executed smoothly as well as quickly.

In your training, remember that snatching your gun out of your holster is only the first step in the draw—the complete training routine must include acquiring your target, shooting to kill, and continuing to shoot to kill until the mission is accomplished. Train like this until the grooves in your muscle memory are deeply carved ruts. And then continue to train for the rest of your life.

It is only "common-sense gun safety" to carry a backup gun. Your backup gun should be instantly accessible by either hand, and you need to train with it both ways. Make sure your backup draw doctrine also precludes covering your own body with the muzzle.

High-risk doctrine dictates a third hideout gun, also accessible by either hand quickly but not necessarily instantaneously since, by definition, it may be hidden in a place you don't normally expose in public.

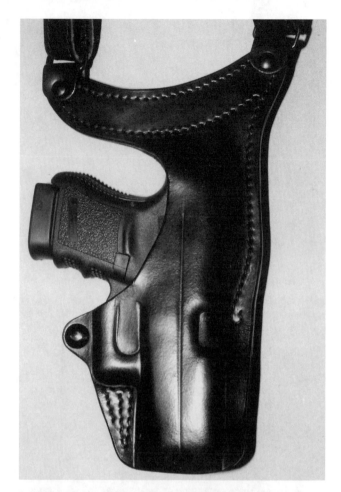

Top: F.I.S.T. vertical shoulder holster overwhelms the little G36, but is great for field use with a large, heavy gun. Photo by the author.

Above: Don Hume IWB holster with reinforced mouth is one of the best. Photo by the author.

For you minimalists, this clip attaches to your gun and clips on your waistband for IWB carry. Photo by the author.

If you're going to carry your gun in a fanny pack, make it so small, fancy, and expensive that it only whispers that you're armed. Photo by the author.

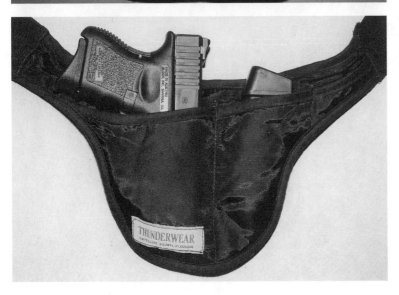

Thunderwear rig fits over your underwear under your pants. It's not quite as uncomfortable as you probably think it is, and nobody's going to stare at your crotch for long. Photo by the author.

Galco pocket holster keeps your gun safe and secure wherever you put it. Photo by the author.

Don Hume ankle holster helps the G27 invade the traditional territory of the J-frame. Photo by the author.

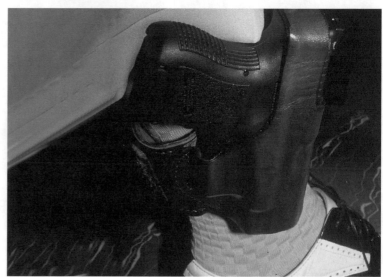

Galco "Concealable" pancake is a comfortable ride. Photo by the author.

Blade-Tech paddle holster is attractively finished, lightweight, stays put on your hip, and provides a smooth draw. Photo by the author.

Sidearmor belt holster is strong, durable, and easy on the draw. Photo by the author.

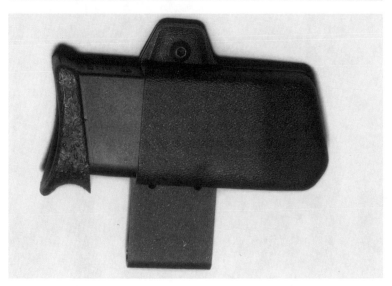

Sidearmor magazine carrier is a well-designed unit that can be adjusted for vertical or horizontal carry. Photo by the author.

Holsters Plus adjustable cross-draw is a must for your limo driver. Photo by the author.

Holsters Plus Sure-Lock model carries big G20 with absolute security while providing instant access. A big hit with cops and hunters alike. Photo by the author.

DeSantis shoulder rig is beautifully made and one of the best. Photo by DeSantis.

It's only "common-sense gun safety" to carry a backup gun.

A fourth gun is arguably superfluous, but an accessible knife is not. Standard carry is the thumb-opening fully serrated Spyderco Endura clip-on, and it's never a bad idea to have another fast-opening or automatic knife in your pocket.

The most common method of carrying the primary gun is in a strong-side belt holster. The backup is often carried over a kidney in a belt or inside-the-waistband holster, but you have to be flexible enough to reach the backup with either hand.

A variation not recommended is carrying the backup at an extreme transverse angle in an "SOB" holster in the small of the back where the grip is unreachable with the off-side hand of any normal person. It's also potentially paralyzing to fall on your back with the steel slide of a gun on your spine.

Double shoulder rigs provide access to either gun with either hand, though the thumb straps can be awkward if you're forced to draw either weapon with the same-side hand.

Single shoulder rigs combined with belt or inside-the-waistband carry are extremely effective, but you have to decide which gun is primary and which is backup and practice with them that way.

A hideout gun can be carried in a holster attached to your ankle, slipped in your pocket, stretched over your underwear, or sewn into a body girdle or wide elastic belt beneath your shirt.

The "Cuban Carry" is a four-gun north-south-east-west arrangement combining a double shoulder holster with both small-of-the-back and underwear holsters.

The "Barko Carry," as it's known in Mexico City, Miami, and northern Arizona, utilizes a

Top: Sometimes a holster is a very simple affair. Bet you can't spot the backup gun. Photo by the author.

Bottom: Your Glock should have a sharp companion. Standard carry is the thumb-opening fully serrated Spyderco Endura clip-on. Photo by the author.

Think of your backup and hideout as spare magazines with guns attached.

single shoulder holster for primary with the backup carried in a perfectly vertical strong-side belt or waistband holster moved around to the off-side kidney where it is very quick to access with the off-side hand, somewhat more difficult but possible to access with the strong hand. This carry places the backup gun in a position normally occupied by a spare magazine, but in this case the spare magazine has its own gun attached to it.

Speaking of spare magazines, if you only carry one gun, carry one or two spare magazines. Not only is this important for increased firepower but, since the magazine is the weakest link in the weapons system, it's critically important for continuously reliable operation.

If you carry multiple guns, things are a little different. Tradition says that all of the guns you carry should be of the same caliber so that all of your spare magazines will fit all of your guns. But if you think of your backup and hideout as spare magazines with guns attached, such consistency may be slightly overwrought. In the age of highly reliable Glock pistols and a multitude of convenient carry methods, there's not a thing wrong with carrying specialized guns of different calibers. In this case, additional spare magazines may not be necessary, though it's always a good idea to have at least one spare magazine for your primary gun.

Excellent choices for concealed carry, both primary and backup, are the .45-caliber G36, the .40-caliber G23 or G27, and the 10mm G29. The hideout gun almost has to be the G27, though some people are built to hide a G23 or a G36 just as well.

•••

HALF A DOZEN FAVORITE SOURCES

Holsters Plus
25727 L Coeur d'Alene River Road
Wallace, ID 83873
www.holstersplus.com
(Innovative Kydex holsters with emphasis on compactness, concealability, and comfort. Glock specialist. Optional Sure-Lock Tab is best ever Kydex holster secure retention system. Featured maker of M-3 tactical light holder. The company is also distributor of Cominolli competition Glock triggers. Owner Bill Smullin definitely makes some of the very best Glock concealment holsters you can get.)

Sidearmor
11029 N. 24th Avenue, Suite 803
Phoenix, AZ 85029
http://sidearmor.net
(Rugged Kydex holsters precision crafted utilizing CNC machining. All holsters can be adjusted for drawing tension with included wrench. IWB holsters feature option of belt loops or J-hooks. Thoughtful designs.)

Blade-Tech Industries, Inc.
3060 South 96th Street
Lakewood, WA 98499
www.blade-tech.com
(One of the leading manufacturers of thermoplastic holsters and sheaths. Holsters have been field-tested at Gunsite and are widely used in law enforcement and special military units. Available in a variety of colors and finishes. I consider their paddle holsters among the best of the breed.)

Snatching your gun out of your holster is only the first step in the draw.

Tauris Holsters
3695 Mohawk Street
New Hartford, NY 13413
www.borg.com/~tauris/
(Tauris owner Mike Taurisano has been a full-time police officer for more than 35 years, and it shows in his handcrafted holsters. Taurisano knows how important accessibility is, and his holsters provide the slickest draw from leather I've ever experienced. The Tauris high-ride Pro Max with reinforced mouth is excellent. And the thoroughly thought-out Tauris shoulder system is one of my all-time favorites. Mike's trademark personal service doesn't hurt either.)

Don Hume Leathergoods
P.O. Box 351
Miami, OK 74355
www.donhume.com
(Specialists in professional law enforcement equipment. Duty, security, and concealment rigs plus all accessories. Traditional craftsmanship and classic designs. Don Hume holsters are built to last.)

Galco International
2019 W. Quail Avenue
Phoenix, AZ 85027
www.usgalco.com
(From its days as the Jackass Leather Company, Richard Gallagher's Galco International has grown into one of the largest holster makers ever. Extensive product line from plain to exotic. Galco makes holsters in every configuration imaginable, including five different shoulder systems ranging from the famous Miami Classic to the original Jackass Rig. I'm still holding my breath waiting for them to offer the Executive, one of the most concealable lightweight shoulder rigs ever designed, for the G36 and G27.)

The Great Glock Watermelon Shoot

10

What you feed your Glock may have a greater impact on your health than what you feed yourself. There was a time when we all fed our pistols a bland diet of plain old hardball because that's what was required to ensure proper digestion. That time is past.

Gun designers and custom gunsmiths have given their new and modified creations a much broader appetite. Bullet designers and ammunition manufacturers have figured out how to make hollowpoints expand more reliably in human flesh even at relatively modest handgun velocities. And some, influenced by the fast company of Lee Jurras and Super Vel some 30 years earlier, have cranked up velocities and operating pressures to take full advantage of the greater strength of newer guns.

Others have devised exotic frangible, or prefragmented, handgun loadings that are almost as devastating at close range as a shotgun blast. The best of these frangible rounds are made by hand, one bullet at a time, so they're expensive. Some say they're too expensive to practice with and therefore shouldn't be counted on in an emergency, but others ask how much the shooter figures his life is worth.[1]

A few friends and I recently took a wide assortment of these current factory loads to the range, including some of my favorite performance loads from Black Hills, Cor Bon, MagSafe, Triton, Hornady, Federal, Eldorado, Georgia Arms, and Winchester, chronographing muzzle velocities and measuring close-range accuracy through a variety of

Glocks, the results of which you'll find in the tables below. Then, bored as we could be from the tedium of carefully shooting paper for days on end, we loaded up a long-bed pickup truck at a country watermelon stand and headed out for the high desert, the results of which you'll also find in the tables below.

All chronographing was done outdoors on warm, clear days using an Alpha Shooting Chrony. Accuracy tests were three-shot averages at 25 feet over a makeshift rest to approach combat relevance, and measured with a pocketful of change to avoid any misleading appearance of scientific rigor.

Irv Stone of Bar-Sto Precision Barrels in California and Bill Jarvis of Jarvis Barrels in Montana were kind enough to contribute custom drop-in match-grade barrels to give us something to shoot for. Master pistolsmith Robert Krone of Boise, Idaho, carefully fitted these barrels to my guns and polished their feed ramps to accept the gaping hollowpoints and exotic loads we were testing.

The watermelon shoot was strictly for fun. And fun it was, especially when we painted faces on the fatheaded fruits and imagined all that pink mist emanating from the liquefied schemes of certain politicians and ex-politicians.

Cautionary Note: The watermelon tests were performed on government-owned property, so the results bear no resemblance to any real-life situation.

The WATERMELON RATING SYSTEM is as follows:

- One star (✶) = a nice clean hole that kills not only the watermelon but whoever may be standing behind it.
- Two stars (✶) = breaks the watermelon into multiple parts and redirects the bullet or fragments thereof to parts unknown.
- Three stars (✶✶✶) = results in a sticky shower of mist-for-brains that scares the hell out of anybody standing in the general vicinity of the eruption.

It goes without saying that a watermelon is not a man, though the water content percentages are on the same scale. Neither is a watermelon a goat, which is the most recent and reliable source of knowledge we have on how to perform the exploding watermelon trick on human beings who really deserve it.

THE STRASBOURG TESTS

This terminal ballistics research project was conducted in secret on live animals in Europe during 1991–1992. The tests were performed, witnessed, and documented by a privately funded group of researchers, technicians, surgeons, veterinarians, and classified military personnel.

During the tests, 611 adult male French alpine goats, each weighing between 156 and 164 pounds, were terminated with handguns. Goats were used because of critical similarities to man in terms of size, bone shattering characteristics, lung capacity, and thoracic cavity dimensions. Goats, like men, are notoriously hard to kill.

Each animal, perfectly healthy, fully alert, and wired with an electroencephalograph to show

G27 - .40-caliber

AMMO	ACCURACY AT 25 FEET	MUZZLE VELOCITY	WATERMELON RATING
Triton Quik-Shok 155-gr. QSHP (factory rated 1200fps)	G27 w/ factory barrel = Quarter G27 w/ Jarvis match barrel = Quarter	1149 fps 1171 fps	☆☆☆ ☆☆☆
Triton Quik-Shok 135-gr. QSHP (factory rated 1325fps)	G27 w/ factory barrel = Quarter G27 w/ Jarvis match barrel = Silver Dollar	1266 fps 1295 fps	☆☆☆ ☆☆☆
Winchester 180-gr. SXT vintage Black Talon (The #9 .40 load in the Strasbourg Tests)	G27 w/ factory barrel = Quarter G27 w/ Jarvis match barrel = Quarter	912 fps 938 fps	☆☆ ☆☆
Winchester 180-gr. SXT Ranger – Law Enforcement	G27 w/ factory barrel = Quarter G27 w/ Jarvis match barrel = Quarter	940 fps 943 fps	☆☆ ☆☆
Winchester 165-gr. SXT Personal Protection	G27 w/ factory barrel = Half-dollar G27 w/ Jarvis match barrel = Quarter	1024 fps 1055 fps	☆☆ ☆☆
Winchester 165-gr. Partition Gold Ranger – Law Enforcement	G27 w/ factory barrel = Half-dollar G27 w/ Jarvis match barrel = Quarter	1036 fps 1060 fps	☆☆ ☆☆
Winchester 155-gr. Silvertip	G27 w/ factory barrel = Nickel G27 w/ Jarvis match barrel = Nickel	1095 fps 1090 fps	☆☆ ☆☆
Black Hills 180-gr. JHP (factory rated 1000fps)	G27 w/ factory barrel = Half-dollar G27 w/ Jarvis match barrel = Half-dollar	910 fps 920 fps	☆☆ ☆☆
Black Hills 165-gr. JHP EXP (factory rated 1150fps)	G27 w/ factory barrel = Half-dollar G27 w/ Jarvis match barrel = Quarter	1044 fps 1088 fps	☆☆☆ ☆☆☆
Eldorado 155-gr. Starfire	G27 w/ factory barrel = Quarter G27 w/ Jarvis match barrel = Nickel	1094 fps 1134 fps	☆☆☆ ☆☆☆
Cor Bon 150-gr. JHP (factory rated 1200fps) (The #7 .40 load in the Strasbourg Tests)	G27 w/ factory barrel = Half-dollar G27 w/ Jarvis match barrel = Quarter	1110 fps 1135 fps	☆☆☆ ☆☆☆
Cor Bon 135-gr. JHP +P (factory rated 1300fps)	G27 w/ factory barrel = Half-dollar G27 w/ Jarvis match barrel = Quarter	1236 fps 1268 fps	☆☆☆ ☆☆☆
MagSafe 46-gr. SWAT (factory rated 2100fps)	G27 w/ factory barrel = Silver Dollar G27 w/ Jarvis match barrel = Silver Dollar	2201 fps 2225 fps	☆☆☆ ☆☆☆
MagSafe 72-gr. Mini-Glock load (factory rated 1940fps)	G27 w/ factory barrel = Half-dollar G27 w/ Jarvis match barrel = Silver Dollar	2018 fps 2061 fps	☆☆☆ ☆☆☆
MagSafe 84-gr. Defender (factory rated 1800fps) (The #1 .40 load in the Strasbourg Tests)	G27 w/ factory barrel = Silver Dollar G27 w/ Jarvis match barrel = Silver Dollar	1680 fps 1750 fps	☆☆☆ ☆☆☆

G36 vs. M1911***

AMMO	ACCURACY AT 25 FEET	MUZZLE VELOCITY	WATERMELON RATING
UMC 230-gr. hardball	G36 = Half-dollar Combat Elite = Half-dollar National Match = Half-dollar	810 fps 850 fps 870 fps	☆ ☆ ☆
Cor Bon 230-gr. JHP +P (factory rated 950fps)	G36 = Quarter Combat Elite = Quarter National Match = Dime	900 fps 953 fps 956 fps	☆☆☆ ☆☆☆ ☆☆☆
Black Hills 185-gr. JHP (factory rated 1000fps)	G36 = Half-dollar Combat Elite = Quarter National Match = Nickel	931 fps 975 fps 983 fps	☆☆☆ ☆☆☆ ☆☆☆

***Box-stock Glock 36 with 3.78″ barrel versus extensively modified, competition-tuned and accurized Colt MKIV Series 80 Combat Elite and a similarly enhanced vintage Colt National Match, both with 5″ barrels.

G36 - .45ACP

AMMO	ACCURACY AT 25 FEET	MUZZLE VELOCITY	WATERMELON RATING
Triton Quik-Shok 230-gr. QSHP +P (factory rated 950fps)	Quarter	920 fps	☆☆☆
Triton Quik-Shok 165-gr. QSHP +P (factory rated 1250fps)	Half-dollar	1125 fps	☆☆☆
Black Hills 230-gr. JHP +P (factory rated 950fps)	Half-Dollar	930 fps	☆☆☆
Winchester 230-gr. SXT vintage Black Talon (The #9 .45ACP load in the Strasbourg Tests)	Quarter	872 fps	☆☆
Winchester 230-gr. SXT Ranger – Law Enforcement	Nickel	864 fps	☆☆
Winchester 230-gr. SXT +P Ranger – Law Enforcement	Dime	868 fps	☆☆
Winchester 230-gr. SXT Personal Protection	Quarter	833 fps	☆☆
Winchester/USA 185-gr. BEB (Brass Enclosed Base – less lead in the air for all of you who have a pistol range in your basement.)	Half-dollar	730 fps	☆
Eldorado 230-gr. Starfire	Dime	805 fps	☆☆
MagSafe 96-gr. Defender +P (factory rated 1760fps) (The #1 .45ACP load in the Strasbourg Tests)	Silver Dollar	1834 fps	☆☆☆

G20/29 – 10mm

AMMO	ACCURACY AT 25 FEET	MUZZLE VELOCITY	WATERMELON RATING
Winchester 175-gr. Silvertip HP (the standard by which other 10mm loads are judged according to many professionals) (The #5 10mm load in the Strasbourg Tests)	G20 w/ standard barrel = Quarter G20 w/ 6" factory barrel = Quarter G29 w/ standard barrel = Half-dollar G29 w/ Bar-Sto barrel = Silver Dollar	1212 fps 1280 fps 1152 fps 1165 fps	☆☆☆ ☆☆☆ ☆☆☆ ☆☆☆
Winchester 200-gr. SXT vintage Black Talon (The #11 10mm load in the Strasbourg Tests)	G20 w/ standard barrel = Quarter G20 w/ 6" factory barrel = Quarter G29 w/ standard barrel = Half-dollar G29 w/ Bar-Sto barrel = Half-dollar	941 fps 986 fps 907 fps 900 fps	☆☆ ☆☆ ☆☆ ☆☆
Black Hills 180-gr. JHP	G20 w/ standard barrel = Half-dollar G20 w/ 6" factory barrel = Quarter G29 w/ standard barrel = Half-dollar G29 w/ Bar-Sto barrel = Quarter	987 fps 1090 fps 933 fps 920 fps	☆☆ ☆☆☆ ☆☆ ☆☆
Federal 180-gr. Hydra Shok (The #7 10mm load in the Strasbourg Tests)	G20 w/ standard barrel = Quarter G20 w/ 6" factory barrel = Quarter G29 w/ standard barrel = Quarter G29 w/ Bar-Sto barrel = Quarter	1048 fps 1094 fps 1005 fps 1020 fps	☆☆☆ ☆☆☆ ☆☆☆ ☆☆☆
Hornady Custom 170-gr. JHP	G20 w/ standard barrel = Quarter G20 w/ 6" factory barrel = Quarter G29 w/ standard barrel = Half-dollar G29 w/ Bar-Sto barrel = Quarter	1291 fps 1299 fps 1165 fps 1190 fps	☆☆☆ ☆☆☆ ☆☆ ☆☆
Georgia Arms 155-gr. Gold Dot JHP (factory rated 1375fps)	G20 w/ standard barrel = Quarter G20 w/ 6" factory barrel = Quarter G29 w/ standard barrel = Nickel G29 w/ Bar-Sto barrel = Nickel	1345 fps 1455 fps 1284 fps 1315 fps	☆☆☆ ☆☆☆ ☆☆☆ ☆☆☆
Cor Bon 180-gr. Bonded Core (factory rated 1320fps) (The #6 10mm load in the Strasbourg Tests)	G20 w/ standard barrel = Quarter G20 w/ 6" factory barrel = Dime G29 w/ standard barrel = Quarter G29 w/ Bar-Sto barrel = Dime	1350 fps 1444 fps 1275 fps 1300 fps	☆☆☆ ☆☆☆ ☆☆☆ ☆☆☆
Eldorado 180-gr. Starfire	G20 w/ standard barrel = Quarter G20 w/ 6" factory barrel = Quarter G29 w/ standard barrel = Half-dollar G29 w/ Bar-Sto barrel = Quarter	965 fps 1005 fps 929 fps 924 fps	☆☆☆ ☆☆☆ ☆☆☆ ☆☆☆
Triton Quik-Shok 155-gr. QSHP (factory rated 1400fps)	G20 w/ standard barrel = Half-dollar G20 w/ 6" factory barrel = Quarter G29 w/ standard barrel = Half-dollar G29 w/ Bar-Sto barrel = Quarter	1315 fps 1392 fps 1290 fps 1277 fps	☆☆☆ ☆☆☆ ☆☆☆ ☆☆☆
MagSafe 46-gr. SWAT (factory rated 2400fps)	G20 w/ standard barrel = Half-dollar G20 w/ 6" factory barrel = Half-dollar G29 w/ standard barrel = Silver Dollar G29 w/ Bar-Sto barrel = Silver Dollar	2490 fps 2645 fps 2413 fps 2402 fps	☆☆☆ ☆☆☆ ☆☆☆ ☆☆☆
MagSafe 96-gr. Defender (factory rated 1800fps) (The #1 10mm load in the Strasbourg Tests)	G20 w/ standard barrel = Half-dollar G20 w/ 6" factory barrel = Nickel G29 w/ standard barrel = Half-dollar G29 w/ Bar-Sto barrel = Quarter	1783 fps 1901 fps 1731 fps 1782 fps	☆☆☆ ☆☆☆ ☆☆☆ ☆☆☆

Vintage .45-caliber Winchester Black Talons still pack a punch. Photo by Morgan W. Boatman.

Three-star explosion erupted when hit with Triton Quik-Shok .45. Photo by Morgan W. Boatman.

Cor Bon is known for pushing the envelope of velocity to good effect. Photo by Cor Bon.

Black Hills makes a reasonably priced line of high-performance ammo. Photo by Black Hills.

This watermelon was wearing a hat. Shot just above the brim, it is now sailing at an altitude of about 40 feet. Photo by Chad Hyslop.

When retrieved, the hat-shaped flying saucer was damaged beyond repair, with the entire back blown out. Inspection crew, left to right, is the author, video director Morgan W. Boatman, and Mike Rose. Photo by Chad Hyslop.

Author was forced to use his 10mm when a rapidly rolling watermelon attempted to escape from the truck. Photo by Mike Rose.

A one-star (☆) load caused profuse, pressurized bleeding from three watermelons simultaneously. Shooter is Chad Hyslop. Photo by the author.

The author takes out three watermelons in rapid fire. Photo by Chad Hyslop.

We painted faces on the fatheaded fruits and imagined all that pink mist emanating from the liquefied schemes of certain politicians and ex-politicians.

brain wave activity and a transducer to monitor blood pressure, was shot through the center of both lungs from a distance of 10 feet with one bullet. The lungs were chosen as the target because, while not the most lethal shot one could make, it is the shot placement most common in military-police defense-type shootings. A variety of modern handgun ammunition fired through service and concealed-carry pistols and revolvers was tested.

The primary standard of measurement was Average Incapacitation Time—the seconds and fractions thereof required for a goat to fall down and not get back up. It should be noted that goats, unlike humans, don't know they're supposed to fall down when they're shot and will not do so until their bodies cease to function.

The Strasbourg Tests confirmed the lethality of large permanent wound channels, or "crush cavities," caused by hollowpoint bullets. Most importantly, the tests demonstrated in convincing terms that the huge temporary wound channels or "stretch cavities" and the enormous system-wide blood pressure spikes created by very-high-velocity, rapidly expanding and/or fragmenting bullets may be the most reliable instruments of swift death short of a bullet (any bullet) planted in the central nervous system.

There is a compelling degree of correlation between the results of these pioneering tests and the results of actual police shootings as compiled and presented by Evan Marshall and Ed Sanow over the years. Strasbourg Test ratings of cartridges, where applicable, are noted in the tables.

No bullet designer since the confidential publication of the Strasbourg report in 1992 has sat at his drafting board without thinking about those 611 French goats. And knowledgeable handgunners who have read the full report tend to develop the habit of chambering exotic

frangibles like the Joe Zambone-designed MagSafes that killed quicker in all pistol calibers than any other round.[2] They may also top off their magazines with a couple of the little poison pills before the more conventional hollowpoints kick in—if they're confident their pistols will work reliably with mixed magazines, as Glocks are known to do.

And the chosen hollowpoints are not simply bullets with holes in the end. Outstanding Strasbourg performers included the tri-partition Triton Quik-Shok, the post-equipped Federal Hydra-Shok, and the El Dorado Starfire, whose flower-like petals unfold as gracefully as in a nature film—all from the unconventional mind of Tom Burczynski. The Quik-Shoks tested were preproduction examples, but this devastating load has been on shelves for some time now. Quik-Shoks expand very rapidly during penetration and split into three substantial bullet segments that continue to penetrate in three directions over an ever-widening area, creating large multiple wound channels of both the permanent and temporary varieties.

There was hardly a top-10 grouping that didn't include modern but more conventional JHP bullets in high-pressure +P loadings from Cor Bon, Remington, and Winchester. Glocks, of course, devour the hottest +P loads as though they were Wheaties. Much of the ammunition we shot up whacking watermelons was not available at the time the Strasbourg Tests were conducted but was nevertheless influenced by those test results.

It should be noted that the very best performances by the most lethal rounds in all defensive calibers—including 10mm, .45, .40, 9mm, .357 Magnum, and even the .38 Special (in 4-inch barrel configuration)—yielded an average incapacitation time of between four and

Unless your enemy is totally vaporized on impact or his central nervous system is shut down, you're not out of the woods

five seconds. Lucky the goats weren't prepared to shoot back, because even a French goat should be able to get a couple of rounds off in four seconds. I know some people who can empty a high-capacity magazine with deadly accuracy in considerably less time, though they're not the kind of people you'll likely be shooting.

The point is, unless your enemy is totally vaporized on impact or his central nervous system is shut down, you're not out of the woods. Lung shots may be easier, but brain shots tend to be final statements no matter what kind of ammo you're using. Training and practice can make them equally fast. And double-taps are appropriate for any social occasion.

It's time for Strasbourg II. What a waste that the Brits slaughtered millions of head of livestock during the mad-cow and hoof-and-mouth scares of 2000 and 2001 without advancing the science of terminal ballistics a single step. Maybe somebody on the continent was smart enough to take advantage of the situation and it hasn't leaked out yet.

One way or another, new live-animal tests need to be done. Watermelons are fun, but that's as far as it goes—and don't think you can eat your targets afterward because when you shoot a watermelon, even if it is left standing, the insides are churned into inedible mush. Ordnance gelatin is fine, but it's hard to tell a live piece from a dead piece. Actual police shootings are a great source of knowledge, but the statistical numbers are low, the variables are exceedingly high, and cops are not allowed to carry exotic or experimental ammunition.

We need more goats. I'm working on it.

•••

1. José Vega of MagSafe Ammo, Inc. was kind enough to send me several hundred rounds in various loadings for .40, .45, and 10mm, which I fired through a variety of Glock pistols with not a single malfunction of any kind.

2. MagSafe ammo was the fastest killer in .380, 9mm, .40, .45, and 10mm. The Glaser 80-gr. Blue Safety Slug was .04 second faster than the MagSafe in .38 Special, and the Triton Quik-Shok 125-gr. JHP was .22 second faster than the MagSafe in .357 Magnum. It should also be noted that Triton Quik-Shok was a scant .08 second behind the MagSafe for fastest killer in 9mm and that .357 Magnum and 9mm were the only two categories in which the new preproduction Triton Quik-Shok cartridge was tested.

Tropical Glocks 11

Latin America, whose legal traditions are based on Napoleonic Code rather than English Common Law, is a mishmash of gun laws. A virtual nightmare, if you will. There is one saving grace, however. Napoleon was a practical man, not an ideologue, and he realized that rules were made to be broken. If you are a man of substance, a man with good connections capable of exerting a certain amount of financial, political, or personal power, there is always a way to get what you want.

Juan Carlos Hidalgo, a friend of mine who works for the Libertarian Party of Costa Rica, reports a few points about Costa Rican gun rights: "All automatic and semiautomatic guns are banned. For other guns, a license and registration is required. Licensing is nondiscretionary, which means that if a license is asked for, it must be given unless the state proves that the individual has a criminal or mental record or is otherwise legally prohibited from owning and carrying a gun. The license must be renewed every two years. In order to obtain a license, the individual must submit to the authorities a psychiatric examination and legal documentation proving that the gun is his, plus attend a weeklong theoretical and practical training class. If an individual is caught carrying a gun without a license, he faces a six-month to three-year prison term. The state maintains a national registry of who has guns and what sort of guns they have. If an individual is caught owning an unregistered gun, he faces three months of community work."

And here's the kicker, which explains the true state of

Max Joseph applies battle-proven techniques developed for the M1911 to Glock pistols with complete success. Photo by TEES Brazil.

All weapons used in this hostage rescue drill were safety-checked four times by four different people before proceeding. In real life, the hostage-taker would now be bleeding daylight through a quarter-inch hole in his forehead. Photo by TEES Brazil.

"Barbecue at the Kids' Prison." During the time Max Joseph was in Curitiba, a riot occurred at a nearby juvenile detention facility. This is an example of what kiddie criminals do to kiddie informers. Anonymous photographer.

Senior TEES Brazil Instructor Max Joseph and "Ca-Ca," a legendary Rio de Janeiro law officer, demonstrate two-man room combat. Photo by TEES Brazil.

owning and carrying a gun throughout Latin America. Hidalgo says, "Despite all that, only a small fraction of private guns are ever registered and few people bother to get licenses from the authorities to carry them."

Latinos have learned a healthy disrespect for their governments, more often than not ignoring unreasonable laws and answering to the higher calling of self-preservation. As Marxist-inspired U.S. politicians seem to gain more power over our lives with each passing day, we *Norte Americanos* may well have to learn the lessons of our Napoleonic-inspired brothers to the south. Despite Costa Rica's government prohibition of semiautomatic weapons, I happen to know there are quite a few Glocks being carried in that very pleasant tropical country. And they are not all semiautomatics.

There's a hard-core gun fraternity in every country in the world. And it takes but a brief period of time in-country to begin to connect with your own species. Max Joseph has connected to the gun culture of Brazil, which remains vibrant despite severe oppression by the antigun socialist government, and the experience has changed his views not only on the nature of half the hemisphere but on the nature of Glocks as well.

THE TROPICAL ADVENTURES OF MAX JOSEPH

Max Joseph, as noted elsewhere in this book, is the founder of T.F.T.T., the first full-time firearms training academy on the West Coast. He is also the senior instructor for the Tactical Explosive Entry School (TEES), America's leading training institute for law enforcement and

Glocks are fluent in all languages. Photo by the author.

military special operation teams, headed by Alan Brosnan (New Zealand Special Air Service), and TEES Brazil, directed by British expatriate and martial arts guru Kevan Gillies. TEES operates out of Memphis, Tennessee, and Curitiba in the state of Parana in southern Brazil training military SpecOps personnel, military police, and civilian law enforcement authorities.

Max is a Marine who has undergone the most extreme training offered by the U.S. Marine Corps, the U.S. Army, and the U.S. Navy and has been an instructor in most of those courses. Operating under auspices of the U.S. State Department's Crisis Response Team Anti-Terrorist Assistance Program as well as independently, he has instructed thousands of foreign and U.S. military Special Operations personnel, SWAT-team operatives, and qualified civilians in the finer points of antiterrorist operations, hostage rescue, explosive entry, close-quarters battle, field and urban sniping, combat handgun tactics, and other advanced weapons skills. Max also performs international VIP protection jobs throughout Latin America, from Brazil to Mexico City, in addition to the security services he renders at certain high-profile Beverly Hills locations you'd better stay away from.

Though T.F.T.T. and TEES both maintain an armory inventory of Glock 19 pistols, primarily for foreign military and police students training in the United States, Max has always been a 1911 man.

On assignment deep in Brazil, Max recently sent me a note, which began, "Looking down at my leg as I sit here in the South America jungle

"After a long day of training the students go out that same night and practice what they've learned in real-life firefights."

writing this to you, I see a Glock .45 in a Blackhawk low-leg rig. Funny how things turn out sometimes."

In daily e-mail dispatches from the bush and in a sit-down conversation on his return to the States, Max told me what it was like training professional Glock operators in a country very different from our own.

"Guns only speak one language," Max reminded me. "Shooters are alike all over the world, in every country I've ever been in. The difference lies in how urgently they regard their training and how quickly they apply it. Here in Brazil the ordinary routine is that after a long day of training the students go out that same night and practice what they've learned in real-life firefights. I've participated in several of those *Chouque Rone* troop operations myself. And just today I was informed that a unit I graduated Sunday was involved in a gunfight in Rio on Tuesday that left seven dead. I didn't lose any students. It's great for an instructor to get that kind of immediate feedback.

"The training these guys get in their military and police academies down here is extremely basic. There are no advanced shooting courses and they learn nothing about tactics. We teach them high-risk patrol, emergency de-busing, counterambush, firing from vehicles, hand-to-hand combat, weapons retention, hostage rescue, two-man team operations, explosive entry, and structure clearing. We have a rambling kill-house that's made up of narrow passageways and alleys just like the high-crime areas in the slums of Rio de Janeiro. It's high-speed training, and the guys can get pretty excited. We haven't had any injuries yet, but I have an air-blast foghorn I use to call an immediate cease-fire, and I've had to use it pretty often.

"Even if their departments won't pay for the training, these guys fork over a month's salary or

more to pay for it themselves. The practice ammunition alone is an outrageous expense because the government controls distribution and no imported ammo is allowed. But our students are eager to learn and they learn fast. The worst thing that happens is that sometimes we get an A-class or Master-class IPSC shooter we have to retrain.

"All of the training we do in Brazil is restricted to military, law enforcement, and licensed VIP protection personnel. No civilians are allowed. The reason for that is because, unlike in the States, street criminals and drug cartels down here actively seek state-of-the-art military firearms training, and we can't be instructing the enemy.

"Brazilian gangs are a thousand times more dangerous and violent than the punks we have in the States. Law enforcement is a prime target— last year, in the city of São Paulo alone, more cops were killed than in the entire United States. You need to watch your back, and it's a nice place to have friends. All of the military and police guys I work with here are totally for civilian carry, and every civilian I know carries a gun. Brazil is a violent country, and it's taught me to appreciate the freedoms we have in the U.S. Down here they all hate what the United Nations is trying to do to them in terms of disarmament. It's a very real threat to their lives and the lives of their families.

"There's no death sentence for criminals in Brazil, not even a life sentence. If you hack a hundred school children to death, the maximum prison sentence you can get is 30 years. But, as you might imagine, 30 years in a Brazilian prison is a fate worse than death. To say that prisoners are not pampered is a vast understatement. There are frequent breakouts, and once or twice a week there are giant prison riots—shooting riots, often assisted by gangs armed with automatic weapons and hand grenades from the outside. Nobody can survive anything like 30 years in a Brazilian

"The Glock 17s and 19s we use are hands-down the most universally reliable pistols I've ever used in my entire life."

prison, so they start planning on how to get out as soon as they get in. Law enforcement has to be in a constant state of readiness.

"All of the TEES instructors and most of the officers we train and most of the students who can afford to buy their own weapons shoot Glocks. The Glock 17s and 19s we use are hands-down the most universally reliable pistols I've ever used in my entire life. I can admit to you now that I love Glocks, and so do the students. These guys are not doing this to collect patches and badges and trophies, they're doing it because their lives are on the line every moment of every day."

FREEDOM FOR SALE

Max Joseph confirmed what I had heard from other operatives in Latin America and in third-world countries around the globe. The United Nations and the Clinton administration had been extorting these countries for years, using the leverage of gigantic loans and foreign aid packages to force compliance with Bill Clinton's bizarre antigun, antifreedom agenda.

The oppressive antigun laws passed by Brazil and other politically vulnerable countries during the Clinton administration—laws that disarmed law-abiding citizens, increased the power of criminals and criminal enterprises, and caused ever-increasing violent crime rates along with the cold-blooded slaughter of countless innocent civilians—were the direct result of Clinton's blackmail policies.

With the demise of America's disgraced traitor, these laws are already beginning to relax, allowing citizens to begin to reclaim their countries from the rule of Clinton-sponsored criminals. Think about that the next time someone says it doesn't matter who you vote for as president of the United States.

The enemies of freedom that infect Latin America are the same enemies of freedom that infect North America—cowardly, deceitful socialist crooks, along with the meek intellectual peasants who follow them, whose greatest fear is a people with the will and the arms to defend their lives and their liberties from the degrading depredations of human parasites, scavengers, and ideological criminals.

Perhaps Latin America is ahead of the game, in that firmly planted in its culture and the unending civil wars that helped produce it is the idea that the requisite final answer to the enemies of freedom is not compromise but extermination.

•••

INTERNET SOURCES

Tactical Firearms Training Team (T.F.T.T.)
www.tftt.com

Tactical Explosive Entry School (TEES)
www.tees-training.com

TEES Brazil (in Portuguese)
www.teesbrazil.com.br

Libertarian Party of Costa Rica (in English)
www.libertario.org/en/

Silent Glocks

12

Powder that burns with a turbulent whimper has an altogether different smell from powder that burns with a loud bang. The lurid scent exhaled by a suppressed Glock is amplified by lack of the auditory overload one normally expects with a trigger press, and the phenomenon quickly becomes addictive. Perhaps that's why the cultural authorities in Hollywood have always considered silencers instruments of the devil, used only by gangland assassins, mercenaries in the employ of corrupt politicians, and CIA types gone bad.

Actually, the feds and government contract shooters use silenced weapons most often to eliminate bothersome furred and feathered wildlife around busy airports and in popular picnic areas of national parks.

Ask any hunter in densely populated Europe, where these evil apparatuses are sold across the counters of sporting goods stores, and he'll tell you that the use of a sound suppressor is but a common courtesy. And a lot of American babies who live in or near rural areas would likely appreciate not having their naps interrupted by the occasional crack of gunfire during hunting seasons, just as they appreciate that the 12-cylinder Ferrari that commutes past their house twice a day is equipped with a sweet-sounding exhaust system and their next-door neighbor finally fixed the rusted out mufflers on his big Ford truck.

The bad rap on suppressors began during the Great Depression of the 1930s, when people often shot meat when they were hungry instead of when Fish and Game

The best revenge is getting what you want. Owning a suppressed Glock is worth the hassle.

bureaucrats told them they could. Well-fed government employees, who used suppressed weapons all the time just doing their jobs along with whatever else they did in the woods, mounted a major effort to have suppressors outlawed for nongovernment use because they were desperately afraid some unemployed poacher might get away with a bag of organic groceries for his family without setting off a high-decibel alarm during the commission of his crime.

Thus one of the most useful devices ever invented by the firearms industry was thrown into the same politically incorrect category as select-fire weapons ("the foundation of Al Capone's criminal empire") and short-barreled shotguns ("the bank-robbers' weapon of choice").

Even the ruling Democrat party of the time could see that an outright ban on these utilitarian enhancements of ordinary firearms would not survive a Constitutional test, so it decided to bring out its most powerful weapon and tax them to death.

Today, most Americans believe that sound suppressors, or "silencers" as they are known in popular jargon, are illegal. In the few states that specifically make them so, they are. In the majority of states, and under federal law, they are perfectly legal to own and use (as are machine guns and sawed-off shotguns) so long as you pay a $200 extortion fee, or "transfer tax," to the federal government. That's on top of the $600 to $1,200 or so you'll actually pay for a good sound suppressor from one of the several companies that manufacture them.

You'll also have to fill out about the same amount of paperwork required to buy a house and sit on your hands for three or four months while some government clerk stares at your fingerprints and reads over your papers and stamps them and hands them off to some other clerk who does the same, and on and on until

they figure they can't get away with stalling any longer. (Hint: If you own or control a corporation, you can have your suppressor transferred to the corporation instead of to yourself personally and thereby *radically* reduce paperwork and waiting time.)

The best revenge is getting what you want. Owning a suppressed Glock is worth the hassle. It's not only one of the most fun toys you'll ever own but a utensil so handy that it comes close to being a practical necessity. It's the "weapon of choice" for discreet animal control, target practice without annoying (or scaring) the neighbors, hunting within earshot of farmers or other local residents, bringing down game without spooking herds of wildlife for miles around, protecting your own ears from hearing loss without having to wear those damned earmuffs, and simple joys like watching watermelons explode as if by magic.

WHY GUNS MAKE NOISE

The ear-piercing and sometimes earth-shaking noise made by a firearm comes from two sources:

- A powerful compression wave is generated by super-heated gases from rapidly burning propellant suddenly blasting out of the muzzle under extremely high pressure into the cold hands of ordinary air, very much like lightning-induced thunder.

  In any conventional revolver, by the way, these gases also escape from even the most minute gap between the cylinder and the barrel, the gap being a necessary condition of their operation. Thus a revolver (despite the wisdom of Hollywood's experts) cannot be quieted down no matter what kind or how many mean-looking silencers you screw on the end of its barrel.

- Continuous shock waves, heard as a sonic boom, are produced by any object moving through the air faster than the speed of sound, whether a jet fighter at 750 miles per hour or a bullet at 1,100 feet per second.

There is nothing anybody can do to silence a sonic boom. The sound, however, is nondirectional, so as much as it may hurt your ears, you can't tell where the sound is coming from. In some applications, the sonic boom is not a consideration since it doesn't give away the shooter's location, though it very definitely signals that there's a shooter somewhere in the area. In most applications, however, the benefit of a bullet that sails silently through the air is as important as a muzzle blast that doesn't make any noise.

Sound suppressor manufacturers, in their attempts to solve the muzzle blast problem while rendering the unsolvable sonic boom problem inoperative, concentrate on firearms that can fire effective subsonic loads, such as .22, .32, .380, 9mm, .40, and .45 pistols. In general, the smaller the bore size the easier the

AWC Systems Technology, whose suppressors are widely used throughout the special operations community, places a recoil regulator between the muzzle and the actual suppressor on precision-balanced autos such as Glocks and Sigs. Photo by AWC Systems Technology.

Gemtech's small but effective Aurora suppressor is designed specifically for government deployment of the diminutive Glock 26. Photo by Gary Gelson.

gun is to silence. Many of these pistols can be silenced to such a degree that the loudest sounds you or anyone else hears when you pull the trigger on a live round are the satisfying thud of your bullet sinking into its target and the mechanical functioning of your pistol's action. The latter is a small racket that can nevertheless be easily avoided, especially on a suppressed Glock.

The muzzle blast problem is solved simply (in theory) by circulating the hot gases through a suppressor "can" where they are cooled, often by water or grease or some other liquid in a "wet can," and allowed a greater volume within which to expand and dissipate pressure before they are released.

Trouble is, the original Browning-designed recoil-operated action utilized by virtually all

major-caliber pistols, including Glocks, doesn't appreciate having a can of water hanging off the end of its nose. Glocks, whose fast slides and lightweight tilting barrels are particularly well balanced, have an especially strong objection to such abuse. Your Glock will take some cajoling before it will go quietly into semiautomatic mode.

THREE PATHS TO SILENCE

Three of the major sound suppressor manufacturers approach Glocks from three different perspectives to achieve similar results.

AWC Systems Technology of Phoenix, Arizona, manufactures a couple of beautifully made suppressors appropriate for Glocks and widely used throughout the special operations

Mark White of Sound Technology simply can't stand noise. He builds his suppressors accordingly. Photo by Sound Technology.

community. For precision-balanced autos such as Glocks and Sigs, the company offers a recoil enhancing device it calls a Recoil Regulator, otherwise known as a recoil accelerator or booster, that fits between the muzzle and the actual suppressor used on Glock pistols. The Recoil Regulator module allows the shooter to adjust the function of his Glock between semiautomatic cycled and locked-slide, hand-cycled modes of fire, depending on the requirements of the situation.

It must be noted that artificially boosting recoil forces beyond original design specifications, which every recoil accelerator does, can be very hard on your gun over time. Reliable semiautomatic cycling in a suppressed Glock comes at a price.

Gemtech of Boise, Idaho, makes a neat and

highly effective little suppressor called the Aurora, which it designed specifically for the Glock 26. The Aurora is the most compact 9mm suppressor on the market and is small and light enough to ensure reliable semiautomatic cycling in the mini-Glock, a virtue that could only be achieved by utilizing "wipe" technology.

Wipes are discs of urethane material that bullets penetrate as they move through the suppressor. As a bullet passes through, the wipes close up to contain propellant gas within the body of the suppressor. Wipes are effective enough to allow a very small suppressor to reduce sound dramatically, but the number of shots you can fire through such a system before you have to replace the shot-through wipes is naturally very limited.

Gemtech's Aurora was designed to cycle

Jonathan Arthur Ciener offers an extended barrel complete with sound suppressor on his popular Glock .22LR conversion units.

about one magazine before replacing the wipes, an operation that is quick and easy with Gemtech's replacement kits but not without a big problem for civilian shooters. The ATF in its wisdom considers suppressor parts, such as wipe replacement kits, to be suppressors unto themselves, requiring an additional $200 transfer tax and paperwork with each part you buy. This would, in effect, cost the civilian shooter $200 for each magazine fired through the Aurora, and that's why Gemtech sells these particular little gems only to military agencies, which are exempt from the wisdom of the ATF.

Gemtech makes other suppressors for Glocks, which do not require this level of maintenance but do require hand cycling.

Sound Technology in Pelham, Alabama, believes the problem of automatic cycling in

suppressed Glocks is not a problem at all but a blessing in disguise. Mark White tells me that what appears to be a Glock disadvantage is actually the opposite because suppressed semiautomatic weapons are more effective when cycled by hand rather than in self-loading mode anyway.

White is a pioneer in sound suppression technology. He is a man who doesn't like noise and so began his childhood shooting career with a ghostly quiet bow and arrow. Since those days, he has demonstrated over and over again that a properly suppressed subsonic firearm can be even quieter. He is the owner and founder of Sound Technology and author of *The Ultimate Ruger 10/22 Manual and User's Guide* (Paladin Press 2000), wherein he explains some of the subtleties of suppressor

If you have to fire a large-caliber unsuppressed gun in a small room or a closed car, you will likely blow out your eardrums. A suppressed Glock comes close to being a practical necessity.

design. Today, he is building more suppressors for Glocks than ever before.

White said, "I view a suppressed Glock as a hand-cycled, repeating firearm, a definite advantage in most serious suppressed-fire scenarios. Hand cycling is always far quieter than automatic cycling because it also eliminates the sound that comes from the open breech during automatic cycling. Hand cycling also totally eliminates the visibly glowing propellant particles ejected from the breech and eliminates muzzle flash as well, both of which can be produced in abundance with automatic cycling. And hand-cycling allows you to capture your spent casings instead of spewing brass all over the countryside."

Retrieval of brass is so important in certain covert military operations that the government actually invented the world's only suppressed revolver a few years back just to address the problem. As you know, a revolver retains its spent brass so you can retrieve it by hand. This gun was based around special ammunition that, on firing, forced a temporary sleeve between the cylinder and the barrel to bridge that normally essential gap so that all the gases would be directed out the muzzle and into the suppressor. One can only imagine how many millions were spent to develop a special weapon that offers the same benefit as a hand-cycled Glock.

Expert craftsmen like those at AWC, Gemtech, and Sound Technology build high-quality, reliable suppressors that seem to work like magic. But the basic theory of sound suppression is so simple that you can build one that works reasonably well all by yourself. There are quite a few books and plans readily available to tell you how to do just that. The reason you probably won't is because the cost of the federal

Special Occupational Tax you'll need to make your puttering legal is $1,000 a year. And the cost of puttering without obtaining said license is a $10,000 fine and 10 years in federal prison. The same penalties apply if you somehow get your hands on somebody else's homemade or professionally built suppressor without paying the $200 transfer tax to the government. These people take their taxation, and their stealth gun control schemes, quite seriously.

At last count, 37 states allowed private ownership of silencers: Alabama, Alaska, Arizona, Arkansas, Colorado, Connecticut, Florida, Georgia, Idaho, Indiana, Kentucky, Louisiana, Maine, Maryland, Minnesota, Mississippi, Montana, Nebraska, Nevada, New Hampshire, New Mexico, North Carolina, North Dakota, Ohio, Oklahoma, Oregon, Pennsylvania, South Carolina, South Dakota, Tennessee, Texas, Utah, Virginia, Washington, West Virginia, Wisconsin, and Wyoming. Of the states that prohibit civilian ownership of silencers, California, Iowa, Kansas, Massachusetts, Missouri, and Michigan allow class 3 dealers and class 2 manufacturers to possess them for sale to the government. Virtually any government agency or municipality in any state may own and use silencers without restrictions.

One thing to keep in mind—if you ever have to fire a large-caliber unsuppressed gun in a small room or a closed car, you will likely blow out your eardrums. You can think of this as an additional self-defense tax demanded not by any criminal invader but by simple-minded voters in your own neighborhood who are just trying to protect you from yourself with "common-sense gun safety regulations."

•••

SOUND SUPPRESSOR MANUFACTURERS

Sound Technology
P.O. Box 391
Pelham, AL 35124
www.soundtechsilencers.com

Gemtech
P.O. Box 3538
Boise, ID 83703
www.gem-tech.com

AWC Systems Technology
P.O. Box 41938
Phoenix, AZ 85080
www.awcsystech.com

Advanced Armament Corp.
221 West Crogan Street
Lawrenceville, GA 30045
www.advanced-armament.com

Capital City Firearms
P.O. Box 29009
Richmond, VA 23242
www.ccfa.com

Jonathan Arthur Ciener
8700 Commerce Street
Cape Canaveral, FL 32920
www.22lrconversions.com

Night Glocks

13

Most showdowns don't happen at high noon in the middle of Main Street. According to statistics from the FBI and every police and sheriffs department in the country, the majority of deadly encounters with firearms occur in low-light conditions—darkened bedrooms, unlit alleys, moonlit city streets, foggy parking lots, hazy saloons, dew-covered backyards, and any number of dark places in the middle of the night.

The requirement to pull the trigger under invisible sights on a shadowy assailant is not well served by training only on clearly defined targets in broad daylight. Criminals are phantoms of the night, and both you and your Glock must be fully equipped and prepared to plant lead bullets in their ghostly hearts and minds.

Every good shooting school includes one or two night shoots, as does any season of serious competition, as does more advanced police training. But that's not enough. The odds are heavy that it will not be a bright summer afternoon with bluebirds singing when you shoot for your life, so you'd better take a little extra time to stack the odds in your favor.

Las Vegas shooters spend more time on the graveyard shift than anybody, and the justifiably famous Desert Sportsman's Rifle and Pistol Club in Red Rock Canyon is where I've done more night shooting than all other places combined. There are a couple of reasons for this. For one thing, Vegas is a 24-hour town, and constant activity is not limited to the Strip. Most importantly, during a large part of

Heinie Straight Eight Slantpro tritium sights are compact but offer high visibility. Photo by Tom Yates.

Heinie rear sight installed on G27. Sights shoot perfectly to point of aim. Photo by the author.

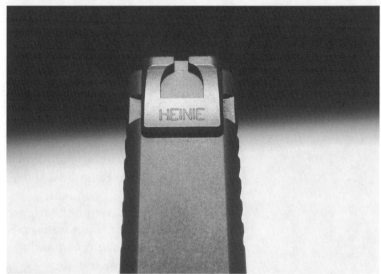

Heinie-designed front sight. Note Trijicon identification. Photo by the author.

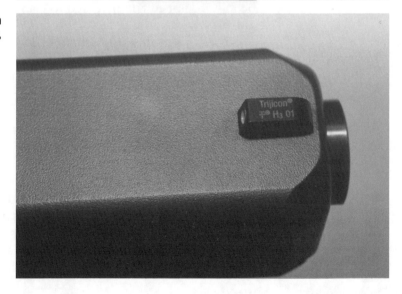

The odds are heavy that it will not be a bright summer afternoon with bluebirds singing when you shoot for your life.

the year daytime temperatures in the Mojave Desert frequently reach 120°F or more, which means you can fry eggs on a cold Glock slide in the shade. Well, you could if there were any shade to be found, which there isn't. Nighttime is often the *only* time you can shoot and stand upright at the same time.

Just because they do a lot of shooting in the dark and relative cool (90° is a cool night in Las Vegas) doesn't necessarily mean that they learn anything from it. I went through an IPSC night match once in Vegas where all of the game-smart shooters wore *miner's lamps* strapped to their heads! Now there's a defensive tactic you can apply on the street. Combine that headlight with a Day-Glo target glued between your eyes and you'll be good to go. And don't we all have miner's lamps hanging on our bedposts? Aren't they offered as optional accessories with those barn-door flannel pajamas some of us used to wear?

IPSC-style idiocy aside, there are some very effective things you can do to help you see in the dark that won't get you shot just because nobody wants to see your defective genes passed on.

TRITIUM SIGHTS

Tritium is a radioactive gas that glows brightly in the dark. It is a crucial component of nuclear warheads, used to enhance the explosive yield of hydrogen bombs. Tritium is an isotope, or radioactive form of hydrogen that actually occurs naturally in the environment, though the amount is too small for practical recovery, so the U.S. government produces it in a complex nuclear reaction process. Tritium has a half-life of a little over 12 years before it begins to fade significantly but is still glowing to some degree after almost 90 years.

Glock shooters insert miniature vials of tritium in their front and rear sights so they can blow up bad guys in the dark. Indeed, no

defensive Glock is complete without this thermonuclear capability.

On a house gun, tritium inserts not only help you see your sights, they help you find your pistol on your nightstand. When you're suddenly awakened by a strange sound, it's comforting to see those little radioactive eyes glowing at you in the dark.

Trijicon, Inc. developed the first tritium-illuminated gun sight legally available to U.S. civilians in 1983, courtesy of an exempt-license granted by the U.S. Nuclear Regulatory Commission. Their first tritium sights for handguns hit the market in 1985, the year before Glocks went on sale in the United States. Other tritium sights are now available, but Trijicon continues to offer the premier tritium handgun sighting system. Trijicons have bodies of machined metal, and the pressurized tritium gas is contained in glass lamps secured in aluminum cylinders cushioned by silicone rubber. The actual little windows through which you view the glowing tritium are made of polished sapphire of startling clarity. Trijicons are built for rugged use, and you can choose green or yellow lamps in a three-dot configuration with all lamps glowing in the same color or in contrasting colors between the front and rear sights. Trijicon makes a full line of its own sights, including systems for SOCOM issue to virtually all U.S. Special Forces Units, and also supplies product to the Glock factory and quality third-party sight manufacturers such as Heinie.

WHITE LIGHTS

Before you level your night sights on a figure in the dark, you have to be certain of who that potential target is or, more accurately, who it isn't. Target identification requires a certain amount of illumination, and you often have to bring it with you—in the form of a hand-held flashlight or a high-intensity beam mounted on the rails of your Glock or, preferably, both.

Very bright rail-mounted tactical white lights such as the popular M-3 Illuminator from Insight Technology not only identify your target but can temporarily blind it and sometimes startle it motionless like a deer in your headlights while you shoot it. But to expand your peripheral vision and improve your depth of field, and to peek into shadows where you don't really want to point your gun, a good hand-held flashlight is as necessary as ever.

M3 Tactical Illuminator from Insight Technology is powerful white light to identify and startle target. Fits on Glock rails. Ideal for house gun. Photo by Insight Technology.

LASER SIGHTS

Laser sighting equipment barely makes it out of the toys-for-all-but-a-few category, which includes the aforementioned miner's lamps and specialized soldiering and 'coon hunting equipment like night vision goggles. But there are practical applications for the high-tech laser as an *auxiliary* sight that are worthy of some serious discussion.

First off, they don't work outside in broad daylight and they don't work at long range. They *could* work in those environments, but the U.S.

Food and Drug Administration doesn't allow it because a laser that strong is a devastating weapon all on its own. Your target would be reduced to a puddle before you had a chance to shoot it.

Laser sights work just fine inside your house even during the day and outside at night at close ranges. In these environments, the laser can be quite useful—but, again, as an *auxiliary* sight, as every laser manufacturer makes clear, because no battery-operated sighting system can ever be considered primary on a defense gun.

You can acquire your target very quickly with a laser. It's a point-and-shoot kind of thing. But the most important feature of a laser sight is that it helps you acquire your target *with your iron sights* very quickly by visually tracing the movement of your sights to the target. This way, you get a proper sight picture with your focus on the iron front sight instead of focusing on the target and the laser spot.

It's comforting to see those little radioactive eyes glowing at you in the dark.

LaserMax laser unit simply replaces recoil spring guide rod. Unit is switched on and off with replacement slide lock. Very discreet. Photo by the author.

The beam of the LaserMax is not continuous but pulsates at rapid intervals similar to a strobe light for high visibility and longer battery life. Photo by LaserMax.

Glock Lasergrip from Crimson Trace is installed at the factory. Photo by Crimson Trace.

Tactical white lights can sometimes startle your target motionless like a deer in your headlights while you shoot it.

If you hunt at night with a battery-operated red-dot sight, an auxiliary battery-operated laser sight gives you a redundant system. And you can sight in the red-dot for longer range, the laser for shorter, and have a simultaneous multi-range system for fun and games.

A laser can be an aid in practicing your trigger control during dry-firing exercises because it lets you see exactly how badly you flinch painted on the wall in front of you. It also helps refine the instincts of any point- or hip-shooters out there.

There are those who say the sight of a laser beam directed at a criminal's heart intimidates him into quick submission. But since you can't see the actual beam of a laser except in a room filled with the heavy smoke of crack cocaine or layers of dust stirred up by heavy boots, in which case the laser beam is usually coming out the front end of an MP-5 submachine gun, I doubt if any auxiliary intimidation is required. The beam does, however, give fellow SWAT team members operating in these conditions a visual cue as to whether a suspect is covered or not.

Laser systems can be as small and unobtrusive as the integral unit from LaserMax that simply replaces the recoil spring guide rod in your Glock. (The pulsating beam of the LaserMax blinks ominously like a strobe light counting down the seconds to liftoff and can, indeed, raise the hairs on the back of your neck if you are unlucky enough to be standing in its path.) Others can be large enough to combine the laser with a white light or anything else your muzzle can bear. I understand somebody is thinking about adding a grenade launcher.

A WORD OF CAUTION ABOUT MOUNTING THINGS ON THOSE CONVENIENT RAILS

When a Glock fires, its polymer frame flexes to an imperceptible degree. On rare occasions, altering the dynamics of that flexing can lead to unexpected results. Like malfunctions. The Glock factory works closely with third-party manufacturers to ensure that this doesn't happen. But, since we all know that individual guns have individual personalities, it is *always necessary* to thoroughly test any add-on equipment on your personal Glock before sending it out on a critical mission.

•••

SOURCES

Trijicon
49385 Shafer Avenue
P.O. Box 930059
Wixom, MI 48393-0059
www.trijicon-inc.com
(Self-luminous sights and scopes.)

Heinie Specialty Products
301 Oak Street
Quincy, IL 62301
www.heinie.com
(Tritium and competition sights for handguns, custom pistolsmithing.)

Insight Technology
3 Technology Drive
Londonderry, NH 03053
www.insightlights.com
(M3 Tactical Illuminator for Glocks and other white lights and lasers.)

Lasermax Inc.
3495 Winton Place, Bldg. B
Rochester, NY 14623-2807
www.lasermax-inc.com
(The world's only totally internal laser sight. User installed. NATO approved.)

Laser Devices, Inc.
2 Harris Court, A-4
Monterey, CA 93940
www.laserdevices.com
(Rail-mounted laser, infrared, and tactical light systems for Glocks.)

Crimson Trace Corporation
8089 SW Cirrus Drive
Beaverton, OR 97008
www.crimsontrace.com
(Lasergrips factory-installed on most Glock models.)

The Enigmatic Glock Trigger

14

The trigger is everything in a Glock pistol. Even more than the Polymer 2 frame and the long list of other engineering innovations, the revolutionary Glock trigger mechanism is the most radical functional departure from the past.

In virtually every pre-Glock handgun, the function of the trigger is simply to drop the external or internal hammer off the sear. The hammer then drives the firing pin into the primer of the cartridge. But a Glock has no hammer, inside or out, and no conventional sear. Pulling the trigger fires the gun, but it also does other things that in traditional guns require additional fingers or thumbs operating separate exterior levers or spring-loaded parts.

GET USED TO IT

For shooters used to any other gun, the Glock trigger takes some getting used to. A great many of the most sophisticated Glock shooters are former and current 1911 shooters. Among them, it's a universal first impulse as they start shooting Glocks to want to change the complex Glock trigger to make it feel like a simple 1911 trigger. It sometimes takes them years to realize that this is not only impossible but a mistake.

To begin with, a Glock trigger is not one trigger but two. When you press the little trigger in the middle of the big trigger you release the first of Glock's three internal safety mechanisms so that the big trigger can move. You can tug and squeeze and pound on the big trigger all day long and the gun won't fire. You have to declare your intent to fire the weapon by placing your finger on the trigger in the firing position so that when you press, the little trigger will disconnect the first safety and allow the big trigger to move. You can think of Glock's trigger safety as performing the same function as the grip safety on a 1911.

As you continue to press the Glock trigger rearward, the second Glock safety mechanism, the firing pin safety, is disengaged so that the firing pin (striker) has potential access to the cartridge for the first time. Until the firing pin safety is disengaged by pulling the trigger a considerable distance rearward, it is impossible for the firing pin to contact the cartridge even if you drop the gun muzzle-down off an 80-story building. Glock's firing pin safety is essentially the same design as the firing pin safety on a Series-80 1911. Competition shooters complained about this additional trigger function when Colt first introduced it in 1983, but after a couple of decades of getting used to the very small change, only the most temperamental of competitors has anything to say about it these days.

Now we get to the good part, the part that bears no resemblance to anything on a 1911 or anything else at all. Whereas the final action of the trigger press that detonates the cartridge in a traditional pistol can be described as a simple falling block, the same action in a Glock is more like a slingshot. The final stage of the trigger press completes the full draw of the firing pin back against its own spring, disengages the third and final safety mechanism so that the firing pin at last has free and clear sailing, and releases it to detonate the cartridge.

SAFETY FAST

A Glock is exactly as safe as the ideal pistol is supposed to be. It will not fire until you pull the trigger with a definite and unmistakable movement. Just as important, if not more so, it will not fail to fire when you pull the trigger because you've made a mistake in the operation of other mechanical controls leading up to the final trigger pull. Glock frames and slides are free and clear of extraneous doodads because the Glock trigger is everything. The smooth Glock slide is itself an important safety feature, as no amount of jostling or rubbing or rough treatment will accidentally disengage any safety device.

The length of the Glock trigger pull from beginning to end is about 1/2 inch, but the final stage that fires the gun is only 1/8 inch. Which means that trigger reset is only 1/8 inch. Which means that, if you train yourself to hold the trigger back during firing and then let the trigger out only until you hear or feel the distinctive reset "click" at 1/8 inch before you press it again, you can fire a Glock at speeds approaching submachine gun cyclic rates.

Glock's seemingly complex multi-function trigger is at the heart of the gun's overall simplicity of operation. Even though the trigger performs several tasks, it is so smartly designed that very few moving parts are required, and those are of substantial size, made of hardened steel, and straightforward in their functions. There is nothing fragile, finicky, or likely to break anywhere on a Glock pistol, including the unique Glock trigger mechanism.

The trigger pull weight of stock Glock pistols is about 7 or 8 pounds, varying slightly from gun to gun, primarily determined by the angled surface of the "connector," which is the crucial part involved in the final release and which requires a nominal effort of 5.5 pounds to activate. This is the way Gaston Glock designed his pistols to function.

You can fire a Glock at speeds approaching submachine gun cyclic rates.

A Glock is exactly as safe as the ideal pistol is supposed to be.

BUT WAIT . . .

As Glocks began to pervade the market of professional and expert shooters, however, two dissenting voices spoke up. Law enforcement trainers faced with inexperienced recruits wanted a trigger designed to resist the heavy-handed techniques of beginners, and departments still in transition from revolvers to semiautos wanted a trigger requiring more effort in the beginning stages to mimic the long, hard trigger pulls of their obsolete Smith & Wesson double-action revolvers. Competitive shooters, on the other hand, wanted a trigger with a lighter final stage to mimic the feathery triggers of their customized single-action autos. Glock did its best to accommodate these specialized shooters, compromising the original trigger design with mixed results.

Glock developed two solutions for the police market. For Miami Dade, Glock engineered a heavier 8-pound (nominal) connector that required some 3 pounds of additional force during final let-off to fire the gun. For New York, Glock developed the very different "New York" trigger, which left the original 5.5-pound connector in place but replaced the coiled-steel trigger spring with a polymer leaf-style spring of unique design, altering the entire feel of the trigger, providing more resistance during the initial stage, and adding about 3 pounds to the overall pull weight. A "New York Plus" spring was also developed, which adds about 6 pounds to the pull weight.

For competitive shooters, Glock developed a connector with a gentler angle, which requires only a nominal 3.5 pounds of effort to activate. The 3.5-pound connector is, indeed, a couple of pounds lighter. But the tradeoff for less resistance in the final stage is a trigger that feels to an experienced 1911 shooter like it has an unfamiliar amount of "creep" in the final let-off.

Glock's efforts to satisfy a wide range of highly opinionated and hide-bound experts opened a virtual Pandora's Box. Suddenly, shooters, armorers, and tinkerers had a variety of trigger parts to play with that could be combined in any number of different ways, some of which the Glock factory specifically warned against, such as combining the 8-pound connector with the New York trigger spring.

Besides the original 5.5-pound connector, there were now an 8-pound and a 3.5-pound connector, and besides the original coiled trigger spring, there were now two versions of the polymer New York trigger spring. By now, third-party manufacturers had also joined the game, offering their own good and bad versions of most Glock factory parts. The mixing and matching soon reached feeding-frenzy proportions, with a multitude of people claiming to have found the perfect combination for the ideal Glock trigger.

AS WE SAID, GET USED TO IT

Those who seek to improve the Glock trigger usually travel full circle—I've seen this time and time again among professional shooters. In the end, after they've stopped trying to make it something it's not, they appreciate the original out-of-the-box Glock trigger as the most distinguishing and distinguished feature of their weapon and develop a full and abiding affection for it. I've made that circumnavigation myself.

Legendary Glock shooter Alan Roy says, "I love the straight-from-the-factory 5.5-pound Glock trigger—the feel and ease of firing and ability to reactivate the trigger so quickly—versus other double-action models like the Smiths and Berettas and Sigs. In my mind, it's ideal for a combat weapon. When you go to the 8- and 12-pound New York triggers, you're just trying to make the release feel like a revolver. I played with the 3.5-pound trigger for a while and, for me,

119

there was no difference, certainly not in rapid shooting."

One third-party manufacturer whose efforts seem worthwhile is Lightning Strike Products of Buford, Georgia. Lightning Strike considers the trigger connector and trigger spring to be within the exclusive purview of the Glock factory, but for other crucial parts in the Glock trigger mechanism—the striker (firing pin), safety plunger (activated as part of the trigger pull), and the trigger itself—they offer well-made drop-in replacements manufactured from lightweight titanium and, in the case of the actual trigger, aircraft aluminum.

The Lightning Strike titanium striker is 60-percent lighter than the factory steel part. This reduction in weight increases striker velocity and decreases lock time about 50 percent, offering potential benefits to long-range accuracy. The titanium safety plunger is lighter than the factory part and has a slightly different profile, promising a somewhat smoother feel during the early part of the trigger pull, though I have found the difference perceptible only by those with extremely sensitive trigger fingers.

The Lightning Strike trigger features a wider trigger safety (the little trigger) and contoured edges on the big trigger that many find more comfortable than the factory trigger for shooting all day long. The Lightning Strike trigger does not alter the factory pull weight in any way but does

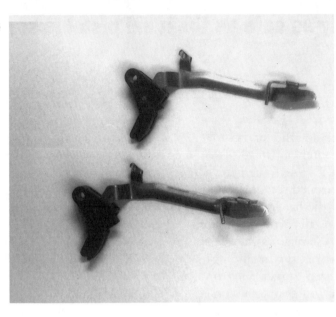

Cominolli competition triggers are almost identical to Glock factory triggers. But not quite. Photo by the author.

reduce the overall length of the initial pull by about 50 percent. Because of the wider trigger safety and the shortened pull length, Frank Karic of Lightning Strike tells me that this trigger is recommended for competition only.

The concept of "competition-only" triggers is, of course, an invention of lawyers trying to protect their clients from fellow lawyers suing on behalf of jerks with empty heads and heavy hands who have accidentally stumbled onto the fact that they are unqualified to operate light machinery. The foundation of the concept, however, is solid enough. In the heat of a real gunfight, gross motor movements tend to override more subtle controls, such as fine manipulations of the tip of the trigger finger, and a more muscular participation on the part of your gun in what you are commanding it to do can have a positive effect on your combat marksmanship. Thus the stock Glock trigger.

Another competition trigger mechanism worthy of note is manufactured by Joe Cominolli of Cominolli Quality Custom Handguns of Syracuse, New York. Cominolli actually makes two different triggers for the Glock, both made up primarily of factory Glock parts with a little magic blended in. The Glock Short Reset Trigger, as the name implies,

Those who seek to improve the Glock trigger usually travel full circle.

shortens the reset of the Glock trigger even more than the already short reset of the factory trigger. In the hands of an expert, unbelievable speed is the result. The second Cominolli trigger, the Glock Competition Plus Trigger, also lightens the pull by a half-pound or so no matter which connector you have installed.

Joe Cominolli is an exception to a statement I made in an earlier chapter that "master gunsmiths can't help you" improve your Glock trigger. Cominolli's quarter-century in law enforcement, his outstanding accomplishments as a member of the prestigious American Pistolsmiths Guild, and his auspicious partnership with master machinist Tom Wallace have produced some outstanding products for both Glocks and 1911s. Among them are the two Glock triggers mentioned, a heavy tungsten guide rod for competition Glocks, and even a foolproof Glock manual safety conversion for more squeamish police departments.

I have installed both Lightning Strike and Cominolli triggers and trigger parts on my hunting-configured G20 and my competition-configured G23, and I like them. These are minute modifications of the original Glock trigger, however, and their value to any individual shooter is subjective.

The Glock trigger is indeed enigmatic to those accustomed to uncomplicated conventional triggers, but it is not inscrutable. It is easy to learn to operate at a very high level of performance and worth every effort to do so because of its unique benefits of speed, consistency, and safety.

•••

SOURCES

Lightning Strike Products, Inc.
4445 W-1 Commerce Drive
Buford, GA 30518
www.lspi.com

Cominolli Quality Custom Handguns
624 Cherry Road
Syracuse, NY 13219
www.cominolli.com

Ultra Glocks

15

Gun owners have always sought to personalize their weapons. The ultimate personalization can be found in telltale notches carved in the wooden handles of old single-action revolvers. Today's integral polymer grips, along with the severe bag limits imposed by modern society, normally preclude such subtle expressions of pride in one's personal gun-handling skills. Short of that, from the ivory-gripped revolvers of Gen. George S. Patton to the lavishly engraved gold-inlaid Colt 1911s and Browning P35s and Walther PPKs I've seen in gun safes around the world to the Star Wars-looking race guns you can find on any IPSC competition course, it's easy to see that we shooters are soft touches for the custom gunmakers' art.

The good news and the bad news about owning a Glock is that third-party manufacturers are in a constant race to provide you with parts and products and services to make your Glock a little different from the rest. My own years of insatiable experimentation have taught me that any material improvement of a stock Glock is a highly questionable possibility, and all attempts to do so must be approached with extreme caution. It is possible for even a small, thoughtless change to adversely affect a weapon that is already perfectly balanced.

That said, there are certain variations on the theme that can be accomplished without doing any harm. In the spirit of Patton (I have no doubt he is wearing a brace of Glocks wherever he may be), some of these modifications can deliver an extra measure of owner satisfaction.

When the late Peter Alan Kasler consummated his romance with Glocks by writing the first comprehensive book on the subject (*Glock: The New Wave in Combat Handguns,* Paladin Press 1992), there wasn't much to say about Glock accessories. The intervening years have seen the booming cottage industry in 1911 parts and accessories peak and a new cottage industry in Glock parts and accessories arise. Even the biggest and slowest aftermarket suppliers rush expanded versions of Glock-specific merchandise to the shelves to coincide with each new model introduction.

There is now a proliferation of Glock gadgets on the market—some potentially useful like grip extensions, some whimsical like barbecue aprons, some potentially perilous like airgun replicas. Glock itself now offers enough logo-laden clothing articles to furnish your entire wardrobe if that's what you want.

The primary off-the-shelf Glock accessories—holsters, sights, lights, trigger components, suppressors, and, of course, ammunition—are covered in their own chapters. This chapter is

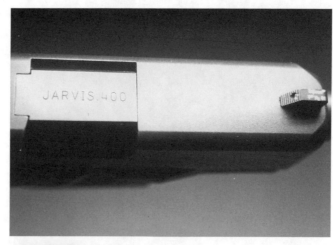

Top: Jarvis match barrel fitted to .40-caliber G27. Photo by the author.

Bottom: Bar-Sto match barrel fitted to Robar-customized G29. Photo by the author.

about another level of Glock personalization, from noteworthy products to one-gun-at-a-time custom work. It is, therefore, suitably short.

MATCH BARRELS

Legendary custom barrel-makers like Jarvis and Bar-Sto bestowed upon the fraternity of competitive 1911 shooters an unheard-of level of accuracy for that weapon, and they have lately turned their technologies and their craftsmanship to Glock.

The accuracy of match-grade barrels can, indeed, exceed the combat accuracy inherent in factory Glocks (though the one-hole accuracy of my personal and particular box-stock G36 with several different kinds of ammo leaves no measurable room for improvement). The tradeoff is that these custom barrels are built with tighter chambers and less forgiving feed ramps and must therefore be hand-fitted to your gun and reliability-tested for the ammo you intend to use. "Drop-in match barrel" is only a marketing phrase and is, in fact, a contradiction in terms. Nor will your new custom barrel be hammer-forged or Tenifer-treated.

Those caveats aside, match barrels from both

We shooters are soft touches for the custom gunmakers' art.

Robar-customized compact .45 with Roboguard finish, grip reduction, beavertail, and other features. Photo by Robar.

The grip on this Robar-customized Glock feels like a 1911. Photo by Robar.

Jarvis and Bar-Sto are works of art finished with beautiful crowns and precision workmanship, true Ultra modifications for Glocks trained to the competition course or the hunting field.

SLIDE REFINISHING

Glock informs me that a quality refinishing job on a Glock slide will not compromise the highly desirable Tenifer treatment of the underlying steel, though any gains realized by such refinishing will be mostly cosmetic. The Robar Companies, Inc. in Phoenix has developed two proprietary finishes that can save the lives of ordinary guns and make Glocks look dressed to kill.

Roboguard is a formal black finish based on polymer technology that Robbie Barrkman, president of Robar, and hundreds of professional gun carriers all over the world claim is absolutely the hardest, most durable, most corrosion-resistant, and all-around best black finish available.

Robar's sporty-looking NP3 finish is a surface

Top: Before and after Robar treatment of the Glock grip and trigger guard. Photo by Morgan W. Boatman.

Bottom: Robar craftsmen can perfectly mate full-size magazines to compact gun for a unique configuration. Photo by Morgan W. Boatman.

treatment combining submicron particles of polytetrafluoroethylene with electroless nickel. NP3 is more consistently and evenly applied than any electrolytic plating, is completely self-lubricating with a very low friction coefficient, and fairly glows with a satin grey/silver beauty.

RECEIVER RESHAPING

The grip shape of the Glock is one of its strong features, but shooters being the cantankerous bunch they are, there is no limit to their desire to mess with things. And polymer is pretty easy to mess with if you know what you're doing. Robar has developed proprietary methods for doing just that—reducing the size of the Glock grip, changing its shape and angle, lopping off that ridiculous trigger-guard hook, building up other areas, adding an integral beavertail, retexturing the whole thing, and just about anything else your cantankerous mind might imagine. The workmanship is absolutely first-rate, performed by certified Glock armorers, and guaranteed for life.

Any material improvement of a stock Glock is a highly questionable possibility.

The author's personal 10mm G29 customized by Robar. Slide work includes additional diagonal cocking serrations. The slide, barrel, and other metal parts are beautifully refinished with NP3. The most functional modifications are of the polymer grip, which is partially reduced, slightly reshaped, and refinished with a nonslip stipple surface. The rounded trigger guard facilitates reholstering, and Pierce grip extensions on the magazines are shaped and finished to blend with the frame so you no longer need worry about pinching your pinkie. The end result is a solid, secure grip on a big, hard-kicking (and gorgeous) gun. It should be added that Robar's quality custom work is not nearly as expensive as you might imagine. Photos by the author.

Jonathan Arthur Ciener Glock .22 conversion unit may be the ultimate Glock accessory. Photo by Jonathan Arthur Ciener.

Components of the Ciener conversion unit are replacement slide, barrel, guide rod, and magazine. Photo by Jonathan Arthur Ciener.

.22 CONVERSION UNIT

The Jonathan Arthur Ciener .22LR Conversion Unit for the Glock 17/22/24/31/34/35 and 19/23/25/32 is included here because it may well be the ultimate practical accessory, transforming your personal Glock into a .22LR practice gun you can shoot all day long for a dollar or two. Ciener is perhaps best known as a Class II manufacturer of automatic weapons, suppressed pistols, and sawed-off shotguns, and the quality for which the company has long been known is readily apparent in these well-fitting and highly useful Glock conversion units. Only a few seconds are required to replace the slide, barrel, guide rod, and magazine. Operation is, of course, direct blowback, and accuracy is excellent. An extended barrel with quick-attach sound suppressor is also available from Ciener for these units (See the Chapter 12: Silent Glocks.)

ULTRA SOURCES

Jonathan Arthur Ciener
8700 Commerce Street
Cape Canaveral, FL 32920
www.22lrconversions.com

Robar Companies, Inc.
21438 North 7th Avenue
Phoenix, AZ 85027
www.robarguns.com

Jarvis Gunsmithing Inc.
1123 Cherry Orchard Loop
Hamilton, MT 59840
www.jarvis-custom.com

Bar-Sto Precision Machine
73377 Sullivan Road
P.O. Box 1838
Twentynine Palms, CA 92277
www.barsto.com

The Glock Underground

16

As you read this, a vast network is operating at incomprehensible speed deep beneath the oceans, over millions of miles of land lines, and through invisible signals passed around and bounced back and forth between high-tech towers on the earth and miniature scientific miracles orbiting the planet. Really.

The Internet is a global command and control center for serious shooters, specialized experts, worldwide professionals, firearms inventors, advanced experimenters, and Second Amendment freedom fighters. It is the source of timely information, hard-earned knowledge, educated opinions, and urgent calls to action. Its labyrinthine arteries are far more extensive and powerful than so-called mainstream media, a communications force that at one time was thought to freely disperse facts and unbiased observations and now is known to deliberately restrict and distort information in the service of an antifreedom agenda.

Even more than Glock itself, the Internet and World Wide Web have changed forever the world that shooters live in. Today, a shooter without access to cyberspace is almost as disadvantaged as a cyberspace traveler without access to a gun. To prove it, log onto the Internet and go to the premier search engine, www.google.com, and type in the keyword "Glock." You'll be presented with an ever-growing list of links that currently comprises more than 180,000 Web sites on your favorite subject.

Most of these Glock Web sites originate in the United States, but some are foreign, with content in German,

More than 180,000 Glock-oriented Web sites are listed on www.google.com. Photo by the author.

A shooter without access to cyberspace is almost as disadvantaged as a cyberspace traveler without access to a gun. Your author's Web site can be found at www.livingwithglocks.com. Photo by the author.

Spanish, French, Russian, and other languages, for which Google often provides instant literal English translations. (Not *good* English translations, but decent enough so that you can gather information you would not have access to otherwise.)

Glock Web sites range from the Glock corporate site to third-party Glock product sites to the most interesting of all—Web sites maintained by individuals and small groups who are dedicated to passing along everything they have ever learned about their black pistols. Most of these sites contain links to other Glock sites, and some include "chat rooms" or discussion groups where you can talk online in real time to other Glock owners around the country or around the world or follow the recorded threads of previous and ongoing discussions about specific Glock subjects.

The Glock Underground is a world of unlimited knowledge and freedom. Some time invested here can be a great support to time invested on the range. Of the 180,000 plus Glock Web sites instantly accessible through your computer, I've listed a few of my favorites, including my own. After that, your itinerary is up to you.

LivingWithGlocks.com
(Glock stories collected from the personal experiences of shooters around the world. Topics from defense to hunting. Product reviews. Interviews with Glock people. Photos. Videotapes. Chat rooms.)
http://www.livingwithglocks.com

Glockworld Magazine On-Line
(Bulletins, Glock vendor ads, other information.)
http://www.glockworld.com/

Jeff Cooper's Commentaries
(Current and archived views on a wide range of relevant subjects from the master of handgun tactics.)
http://www.dvc.org.uk/JeffCooper/

The Official Glock Web Site
(Specifications and photos.)
http://www.glock.com/

Lone Wolf Distributors
(Extensive source of Glock OEM parts and aftermarket accessories.)
http://www.lonewolfdist.com/

Glock Talk
("Chat Rooms" for Glock people in specific subject categories.)
http://glocktalk.com/

Keepandbeararms.com
(The most dynamic, thorough and hard-core website for Second Amendment freedom-fighters. Daily news briefs and links.)
http://www.keepandbeararms.com/

Crazy Mike's Glock Page
(A wild assortment of everything from hard information to humor.)
http://id.mind.net/~micro/glock/index.htm

Sickboy's Gun Collection
(For the full-auto Glock fan. Photos and more.)
http://www.starsol.org/ericl/guns/

Glockmeister
(Glock products galore.)
http://www.glockmeister.com/

Taylor Freelance
(Competition-oriented Glock products, information and database.)
http://www.seattleslug.2alpha.com/

The Glock FAQ
(Answers to "Frequently Asked Questions" plus model info, pictures, commemoratives & collectibles, maintenance tips and more.)
http://glockfaq.com/

The Glock Pages
(Plenty of Glock facts presented by a federal police officer who is an ardent Glock enthusiast.)
http://members.tripod.com/~Glock_Guy/index-2.html

World of Glock
(Interesting information, including industry news.)
http://members.aol.com/SCBLA/WorldoGlock.html

Glock Resource on the Web
(Very complete site loaded with excellent information.)
http://www.glock-guns.com/

Glock Picture Page
(Exactly what it says it is.)
http://www.jpcorp.com/glock/

Internet Shooting Directory
(Links to firearms organizations of interest to all Glock shooters, including competition associations, concealed carry groups, and state organizations.)
http://www.pla-net.net/~rcomer/organ.htm

Talking Glocks 17

ALAN ROY, FASTER THAN A SPEEDING BULLET

Alan Roy pilots a corporate LearJet-60 out of Dallas these days, but his reputation for speed was established a few years earlier when he was an instructor at T.F.T.T. in California.

Alan and his Glock 17 would race against submachine guns like the H&K MP5 with astounding results. It was not unusual to see Alan draw his G17 and place 20 rounds in the A-zone of the target 10 feet away from him in about three seconds, thereby proving that an express delivery of 9mms can be a very effective man-stopper, you don't need a race gun to win a shooting match, and the trigger reset on a Glock can't be beat.

Alan became a living legend in the Glock world one summer night during an advanced T.F.T.T. tactical rifle class. Twenty students, armed with AR-15s and M1As, had leveled their 100-yard steel silhouettes, and the chief instructor, Max Joseph, came up with a final exercise. Someone had left a small can of spray paint sitting beside one of the distant steel targets. For each student in turn, Max illuminated the can with a spotlight for three seconds only, allowing each rifleman that much time to take his shot at the little can 100 yards downrange. The .223s and .308s finished their pursuits and the can still stood.

Alan walked up to the firing line, his Glock 17 strapped and snapped firmly down in his Galco Fed Paddle. Max hit the switch, Alan drew from the secure holster and fired one

Jet pilot Alan Roy is one of the fastest Glock shooters on earth. Photo courtesy of Alan Roy.

shot, and everyone saw the distant can explode into shrapnel before the spotlight's three seconds expired and the night returned. Thus Alan Roy became a permanently highlighted entry in the growing T.F.T.T. book of legends.

I asked Alan about his long-term relationship with his Glock.

"I bought my Glock 17 in 1987, a few months after they were on the shelves, and I'm still shooting the same gun—322,000 rounds later. That includes five years as an instructor; innumerable IPSC, GSSF, SOF, and law enforcement matches; many hours of solid shooting in advanced training courses; and countless professional assignments. At 267,000 rounds I replaced the extractor. It was functioning perfectly, but the corner was chipped and I was going on a major executive protection

gig, so I replaced the part. The only other part I ever replaced was the locking-block pin. It came apart in three pieces once when I punched it out to disassemble the gun, otherwise I would never have known it was broken because there had never been a malfunction.

"When the little subcompact model 26 came out I rushed right out and bought one of those to use as a backup. Even with the shorter barrel, you can still shoot man-size targets at 100 yards accurately. Lately, I've been taking a serious look at the new single-stack .45, the model 36, but I have no intentions of retiring my original 17."

Alan was born in San Antonio and grew up shooting a variety of handguns. The first he ever owned was a .38 Colt Police Special. He started winning shooting matches when he was 14. He mastered the M1911 in the U.S. Marine

"I bought my Glock 17 in 1987, and I'm still shooting the same gun—322,000 rounds later."

Corps, where he gained some other useful skills as an MP and narcotics dog handler. He decided to switch to a Glock the instant he held one in his hand.

"I'd heard about this polymer pistol that was out there. At the time, my carry gun was a Colt Officer's Model, and I had a Government Model and a Smith & Wesson 686 with a six-inch barrel. I went down to Turner's Sporting Goods, which I think is no longer in business, picked up this Glock 17, and it was ergonomically perfect. Damn good weight and size. Just felt right. I loved the balance of the gun and the rapid reset of the Glock trigger.

"The only modifications I've made to the 17 is to put an extended magazine release on it. I tried an extended slide stop but didn't like it. I use Trijicon sights, and I black out the white outlines around the tritium inserts. I've used the same Galco Fed Paddle hip holster for about the last 10 years—it's awesome for comfort—but I'm going to do some experimenting with Kydex holsters soon because of the weight factor. I carry the 26 in a Galco Yaqui Slide around in back where I can access it with either hand. For ammo, I usually shoot Federal 124-grain jacketed hollowpoints. But I still have quite a few pristine boxes of Black Talons left, and that's what I actually carry in both Glocks.

"As far as training goes, mind-set is definitely the most important thing—how you make decisions on a minute-by-minute or second-by-second basis. T.F.T.T. is an exceptional place for that—where you get both mind-set and firearms skills training. You learn to fight, and you learn that when you go to a fight you go there to *win* the fight. All the best schools—T.F.T.T., Thunder Ranch, Gunsite—have parallel philosophies, but the training techniques are a little different."

Having seen Alan perform some pretty amazing feats of both speed and accuracy, I asked him about the relationship between the two.

"Speed and accuracy are about equally important—they have to meet at some point in the middle—but I think accuracy weighs a little heavier. By all means, get your accuracy down and then increase your speed. The accuracy must be there before the speed can come. If you attempt to do it the other way around, you'll be a really fast miss.

"Like we always say at T.F.T.T., the first shot is the one that counts. Unfortunately, too often in competition and on the street, it doesn't necessarily happen that way. We see 50 shots being exchanged at 30 feet and nobody being hit.

"I think the biggest problem with law enforcement marksmanship is officer disinterest. There are a lot of officers who get out there and do their jobs, and then they go home and put their guns away. They go to their required training, and they go to their required qualifications, but they don't do anything else.

"Civilians tend to take their training a lot more seriously than most cops do. There are exceptions, of course. We've both competed against some incredibly good law enforcement shooters, but they are definitely the exception. For the most part, only when you get up into the elite squads, the SWAT and HRT teams, do you see the advanced level of firearms training we should be seeing. Not that you have to teach every cop how to operate an MP-5, but we should definitely step up the training more than just sitting them on the square range and that's it, and there are still departments out there that do that. When the transition from revolvers to autos took place, they just had more rounds to miss with. That was true then, and it's still true today."

I asked Alan how he felt back in the '80s when he was often the only person on the range shooting a Glock.

"I felt fast and accurate. The biggest argument was about the inferiority of the 9mm

137

"One person with a gun who knew how to fight and had the courage to fight could have saved all those lives. I believe each and every responsible individual has both the right and the duty to carry a firearm."

round. They said, I'd rather shoot them with a .45. And I said, Yeah, but I can shoot them three times with a Glock faster than you can shoot them one time. They asked, Why would you want to carry a piece of Tupperware around? But look at all the manufacturers now that have polymer products. Every single one of them has tried to copy Glock and is making polymer-framed guns now.

"Glock was a big bang in the gun industry—as big a revolution as the 1911 was in its time. I'm happy to see that Glock has become the premier law enforcement weapon. Every time I see an officer today, he's carrying a Glock. It makes everybody a little safer."

Alan spends most of his days traveling 600 mph at 40,000 feet, but he's never left his foundation. He keeps his firearms skills honed and his mind-set intact.

"I'm one hundred percent for civilian carry. It's a personal duty in today's society. The Killeen massacre took place not too far from here, and we should all remember that—one person with a gun who knew how to fight and had the courage to fight could have saved all those lives. I believe each and every responsible individual has both the right and the duty to carry a firearm.

"Obviously, you're going to get some people who say they want to carry a gun and then when the day comes to fight with that gun they may not be up to it. That's where mind-set comes in. In Texas concealed carry classes, they spend about two hours trying to talk those kinds of people out of carrying a firearm. They emphasize the legal responsibilities and keep asking them if they're sure they're ready to shoot somebody.

"At the end of the day, I think carrying a gun

is a fundamental and necessary thing—in this country and in society as a whole worldwide."

LT. DALE WOODCOOK, AT HOME ON THE RANGE

Lt. Dale Woodcook is the range master, chief firearms instructor, and operational support commander of a 425-person sheriff's department in the Northwest. A shooter since childhood, he's a lifelong hunter, veteran of the Seventh Marine Regiment in Vietnam and winning NRA competitor, and pioneering instructor of concealed-carry classes for civilians. Woodcook has been on the job for 30 years, including a stint on the SWAT team where he was awarded a Distinguished Service Medal, and is one of the few men on the department who has killed a bad guy in a gunfight.

The politically correct term for bad guys these days is *threat*. "If it was as simple as shooting bad guys," the lieutenant reminded me, "we could just bring 'em in by the carload and line 'em up against the wall."

The particular threat Woodcook had in mind began as an extremely dangerous barricade situation, and when the armed felon came out it was not to surrender. He was distracted for an instant as he drew down on another officer, and Woodcook slipped right through the small window of opportunity, planting a double-tap in the criminal's sternum so precisely that both bullets plowed through the man's vital organs and shattered his spine. The threat was immediately terminated. And so was the bad guy.

"We teach accuracy," Woodcook told me. "It's important to be able to hit the target. It's been my observation that people who can shoot accurately do better in real shootings. In every fatal shooting we've had during my time here, no more than two shots have been fired and every round was a fatal one. There have been no misses. Good training just takes over.

"We have firearms training four times a year. I wish we could do more, but given budget limitations, overtime, taking officers off the street, and other realities of life, we're not going to. We do night shoots. You can shoot a gun accurately in the dark with night sights. You still need a flashlight to light up the threat and identify the target. A drill we use that works great is to light up and identify the target, then shut the light off and move, acquire, and fire.

"Our training is getting more and more combat-oriented. A lot of our training has a specific performance objective. For example, you have to shoot 85 percent to qualify and we're very strict about it. Only 2 percent of our officers don't qualify the first time.

Top: Lt. Dale Woodcook is one of the many law enforcement professionals who are strong advocates of civilian carry. Photo by the author.

Bottom: Glock pistols make a training officer's job both easier and more effective, says Woodcook. Photo by the author.

"We do a lot of training with dummy rounds, you know, mixing the dummy rounds with live ammo. When you hit a dummy round, you have to do a clearance drill—tap and rack. And, of course, you can see if you're flinching or jerking the trigger every time you pull the trigger on a dummy round. And the instructor can see it too. One guy came off the range last year when we did that and he said, 'We should have been doing this for 20 years.' I said, "I've been telling you for 20 years you jerk the trigger.' They're so embarrassed when they jerk the trigger and we see it, they start concentrating on that good trigger squeeze. It's a great training tool.

"When we shoot strings for speed, we train on Glock's very fast trigger reset. I think that's one of the best features of the gun. You know, you hold the trigger back as the gun fires and the slide recycles the action and then you let the trigger out just until the click and immediately fire again. You can shoot so fast and so accurately that way it's hard to believe for guys who are used to other guns. It can make a difference of 15 points in their score."

The Ada County Sheriff's Department has been shooting Glocks since 1998, when the department convened a selection committee to choose a new weapon to be used throughout its divisions. Eight firearms-sophisticated officers were on the committee with Dale Woodcook.

"We were issuing two kinds of guns at the time—a 9mm Smith & Wesson 5906 and, if you can believe it, a Ruger 9mm—neither of which was satisfactory, so a lot of guys were carrying their own guns. We wanted to go with one gun for everybody.

"At first, I wanted to go with SIGs. But you know what amazed me? You know who on the committee wanted Glocks? All the 1911 guys—they all said, 'If I can't carry a 1911, I want a Glock.' And those 1911 shooters, the master shooters, are a hard sell. The guy who runs the state police wouldn't even talk about Glocks for a long time. Now he talks about them, and he smiles when he talks about them. It's because Glocks are so user-friendly, they're the essence of simplicity, and they always fire.

"It's real hard to select a gun without aggravating a number of people. I was absolutely stunned that, in a department as big as ours, we got practically zero complaints about the Glock.

"Now that I've had a Glock, I like it so well that I went out and bought myself another one. We issue everybody a .40-caliber Glock 22, and I have a model 19 I use to shoot up all the leftover 9mm ammo we have.

"Everybody in the department who carries a gun gets a Glock 22 and 155-grain Gold Dots. Our duty holsters are Safariland triple-retention. If you're on plainclothes assignment you can carry your 22 or you can buy your own 23 or 27, and you have a lot of flexibility in your choice of holsters—a lot of our detectives are using Kydex holsters of various brands now, including the Glock-made holsters, because they're so light and thin and concealable and offer plenty of security in a concealed-carry mode.

"When you're off-duty you can carry any Glock you want. I carry my 9mm model 19 off-

duty because I just like the gun; I like to shoot it. My kids shoot it, my wife shoots it. Now, if it's a gun I'm using at work, where I may have to go offensive, where I may have to go kick somebody's ass, where I have to get in and fight and I can't walk away, I like the more powerful model 22.

"We don't have 9mm guns anymore, but we have a lot of 9mm ammo left over. When I or any of my guys go to school—like to NRA Tactical Handgun or Glock Instructor's Workshop—we usually shoot a Glock 17 or 19 to use up that ammo.

"The city and state police departments are switching over to Glocks too. Right now, the city carries double-action-only Smith & Wesson .45s, and the problem they have is that some of the women have a hard time with that long trigger stroke. I think they're going to give them the option of Glock .45s or .40s, and I think the .40 is the perfect trade-off. You have a lot more punch than a 9mm, but with more magazine capacity than a .45."

As with most professionals, Woodcook's embrace of the Glock pistol comes from decades of broad and intensive experience with other handguns.

"I bought my first pistol when I was 21. It was a Browning Challenger. I shot my first 1911 in the Marine Corps. I carried a 1911 for a while when I was a detective. We issued Smith & Wesson revolvers here until we went with autos. We started with the Smith 5906 and I still have one, but I rarely shoot it because I find it cumbersome after shooting a Glock. I have shot and carried everything. When I go to the various Western-states academies I'll see everything. But if I'm going to teach a young person to shoot, I'd rather have them shoot a Glock.

"The first time I saw a Glock I said, 'This can't be real. No, this can't be real.' We laughed at plastic guns just like, in the Marine Corps, we laughed at the first M16s. But once I started shooting the Glock, I realized how accurate it was and how easy it is to carry—it's *the easiest carrying gun.*

"If, in the beginning, somebody had said to

"The guy who runs the state police wouldn't even talk about Glocks for a long time. Now he talks about them, and he smiles when he talks about them. It's because Glocks are so user-friendly, they're the essence of simplicity, and they always fire."

me, 'Before you get ready to retire, you'll be shooting a plastic gun of foreign manufacture, with the safety in the trigger and no hammer, using .40-caliber ammo, and you'll have a computer in your car to run instant criminal record checks, and, by the way, you'll be buying water,' I would have told them they were crazy on all counts. But if you're going to do 20 or 30 years in law enforcement, you'd better have some resiliency and be able to change."

Woodcook's enthusiasm as a Glock shooter is exceeded only by his enthusiasm as a Glock instructor.

"I really appreciate it as an instructor—safety training is simply *Keep your finger off the trigger.* We, all the instructors, were just amazed at how easy it was when we all went with Glocks. No more going up to guys and saying, 'Remember to drop the hammer when you change barricades,' or 'Stop riding the de-cocker,' or any of that. It was much easier to watch what was going on.

"And the accuracy of the things! We have a steel upper-torso target 140 yards from the line. We shoot it all the time. I was shooting it with my 9mm the other day in a strong wind. Ding, ding, ding.

"I had a county commissioner up there, a woman who had never fired a gun in her life. I took her to the 7-yard line and she made this tight pattern with my Glock. I moved her back to the 25 and she never missed. I let her shoot at the 140-yard steel and, out of one magazine, she hit it four times. Instructors like to see that.

"We've had Glocks break. But we never knew it at the time because the guns just kept going. Even when something does break on a Glock, we can fix it right there—no giving it to an armorer to work on for a few days. That's a really

important thing on a combat gun—how easy they are to fix.

"Our Glocks are stock out-of-the-box guns with no modifications. I heard about a kid the other day who had his Glock all loaded up with aftermarket parts—a big old light with a holster for the light and everything—and he was getting malfunctions. I have to believe there are people in Georgia and Austria who know better how this gun works than I do. We shoot them as they come, and we have absolutely no problems. If we get a failure on a Glock, it's usually shooter-caused. If they're properly maintained and lubed like Glock says to lube them, they don't quit. Every time we shoot a line it's about a thousand rounds, and we'll go line after line after line with no malfunctions of any kind.

"When we first went with Glocks, there was this one instructor who was a Ruger fan, if you can believe there could be such a thing—it stuns me. So he had his Ruger and I gave him a brand new Glock and said, 'Go shoot this and get yourself qualified.' Well, I keep seeing he's carrying his Ruger and I say, 'Look, I can make this an order if you like. Well, he was not going to carry any foreign-made plastic gun, so he figures he'll get me. He goes to the range with a bunch of ammo and he snatches the Glock right out of the box and fires about 400 rounds through it—didn't clean it, didn't lubricate it, didn't even give it a chance to cool down. He just kept shooting it, and the gun did not miss a click. He tried to shoot it and shoot it till it didn't work, and he couldn't do it. So he decided he might as well clean it and carry it. Now he's been to the Advanced Armorer's School and he's one of Glock's biggest fans."

On his own time, Woodcook and his second-

141

in-command, Sgt. Larry Roberson, teach a free class to civilians on concealed carry. They've been doing it for 10 years, and it has become one of the most popular programs the sheriff's department offers to the community.

"You hear the hue and cry that if we have gun permits for civilians we're going to have a lot more shootings. Of course, that has turned out not to be true. In fact, it's just the opposite.

"There are 10,000 concealed carry permits in this county, and this year we'll have about 1,000 people go through our class. They don't bring their guns; they get their shooting skills from other organizations. This is a classroom, and we talk about some of the same things we teach in the Academy.

"We talk about our Glock pistols and how we train.

Top: Detective Jim Gardner says he shoots higher scores with his little Glock 27 than with anything else. Photo by the author.

Bottom: Commemorative Glock 17 was presented to Det. Jim Gardner's brother, Deputy Clint Gardner, for his distinguished work on the Security Team at the 1996 Olympic Games in Atlanta. Photo by the author.

We talk about the law. These laws are made by lawyers and politicians—you and I could sit down in 15 minutes and make better laws—but they're the ones we've got. Larry talks about safety—if people would follow basic safety procedures, there wouldn't be any 'mothers march.' And then I get up and talk for about an hour or hour-and-a-half about the use of deadly force.

"I tell them that, unless it's the last thing you can do to save your life, shooting somebody is more trouble than it's worth to you. We take the romance out of killing people. But there are times when you have to.

"I show a clip of a movie about a woman who's accosted by a home intruder. She can't pull the trigger on the guy, and he overwhelms her. I explain that there are three things you need to fight—you need a weapon, you need ability with that weapon, and you need the will to use it.

"You've got to be able to pull the trigger on another human being. You need to sit down and think about whether you can do that or not. This is not TV, where you shoot somebody to death and everybody goes for pizza afterwards. When you actually kill somebody, it's a major emotional event. I know that from personal experience.

"The reality is this—sometimes, when you pull a gun on somebody, they're not impressed. They keep coming. You've got to be able to do it, to fire, to kill them. You've got to have the will to fire, and you've got to know when to do it. Our goal is to teach citizens how to shoot somebody and walk away from it—legally, financially, and emotionally."

On the private citizen's right to carry a concealed firearm, Lt. Woodcook's final words tell it all.

"Personally? I wouldn't go for a leisurely walk on the greenbelt without a piece."

DETECTIVE JIM GARDNER, REVOLVER MAN

Detective Gardner works Crimes Against Persons in Idaho's largest sheriff's department. He first entered law enforcement in Chattanooga, Tennessee. Before that he was a Marine sergeant and gunner on helicopters over Vietnam, where he developed a close personal attachment to his .50-caliber machine gun. Gardner is a lifelong hunter and, over the years, has spent as much time as he could with his rifle stalking the mountains of Idaho and Colorado. On the street, Gardner carries a little Glock 27 with which he is exceedingly happy—much to his own surprise.

"I was always a revolver man," Gardner says. "I bought my first handgun when I was about 16—a nine-shot top-break Harrington & Richardson .22 that was already pretty old and well-worn when I got it. I made my own holster for it in crafts class in high school and practiced quick-draws until I shot myself in the leg. In the Marine Corps we had the option to qualify with a .38 revolver or the .45 automatic. I chose the revolver. I was always kind of afraid of autos—I'd heard they were inaccurate, hard to shoot, and unreliable. When I first got into law enforcement

we all had revolvers—mostly Model 19 Smith & Wesson .38s. And I had my own Colt Detective Special. When we finally switched to autos, we were issued Smith 9mms, and a lot of us were not too happy about that.

"Then, about three years ago, we all got .40-caliber Glocks and I changed my mind about autos. It was the first auto I ever had a positive attitude about. I went through the whole learning process about Glocks, about how much more dependable they are than autos had been before. You can't hardly make them jam up on you no matter how hard you try. And now that I've learned to shoot them and understand them and am familiar with them, I have total confidence in them.

"I've done a lot of shooting with Glocks in 9mm, .40, and .45. In fact, I went out and bought my own pair of Glock .45s—the department was okay with that at the time. They were two different sizes, and I liked the idea of being able to interchange the magazines between the large one and the small one. For some reason, I think I shoot better with a .45. And I helped my father-in-law buy a Glock 9mm. That's a real sweet-shooting little gun.

"When the .40 became mandatory we were issued Glock 22s and I bought my own 27. I like the .40s just fine. I qualify with both of them, but it seems like I shoot better with the smaller one. I don't have time to shoot enough to be as good as I can be. When I shoot qualification, earlier in that same day I go through one of those little exercises of putting some dummy rounds in there to solve my flinching problem and I can shoot pretty good.

"I like Glocks because I shoot well with them, they're comfortable, they're light compared to other autos, they're really easy to take apart and clean, and they're fun to shoot—I wish I had more time just to shoot them."

"There are three things you need to fight—you need a weapon, you need ability with that weapon, and you need the will to use it."

"I'm glad there are a lot of people carrying concealed—they might be my backup someday."

Jim Gardner has seen police training improve markedly during his 20-plus years on the job.

"It's important to make things realistic. Like the military says, 'Train like you fight.' If you're out there shooting one way and then you get into a real situation and you go into that firefight mode and you start doing what you've been trained to do, if it isn't designed to help you survive a firefight, you're probably going to . . . die. We shoot realistic scenarios now, and we talk about it afterwards, have a debriefing or after-action review, so you learn what you could have done better, what you did wrong, what you did right. That's good stuff."

Gardner has been in only one police shooting. He didn't shoot but he got shot at—and has the bullet framed on the wall beside his many medals and ribbons from Vietnam to prove it. "Obviously," he said, "I didn't have the opportunity to shoot back or I would have."

I asked Gardner what he thought about civilian carry, and he expressed some surprise that I had even asked.

"I believe in our right as Americans to bear arms. Civilians should be able to carry weapons the same as law enforcement. I think background checks are okay. There are some people out there I would just as soon not carry weapons, but the problem is those people are going to anyway. Just like this Brady Law thing—would that have ever prevented the president from being shot? God, no, absolutely not.

"I'm glad there are a lot of people carrying concealed—they might be my backup someday. There are a lot of good citizens out there, responsible people who carry weapons. They might save my bacon one day, or somebody else's."

The Glock State of Mind

18

People who live with Glocks believe in three fundamental truths. God created man. Sam Colt made them equal. Gaston Glock made some more equal than others.

It is not difficult to see the ghost of John Browning hovering over Mr. Glock's 21st century workbench, one genius encouraging—if not assisting—the other in the creation of a post-*Bauhaus* beauty designed to deliver an uninterrupted series of lethal blows to internal human organs in the name of justice and victory over subjugation.

The Second Amendment is not about duck hunting, and Glock pistols are not about Sunday afternoon plinking or gentlemanly target shooting. These guns are built to save lives, many lives—lives under attack by powerful forces driven by the will to kill.

The beauty of a Glock pistol is not the classic racing-sloop beauty of a Browning High Power but that of next year's Mercedes-Benz, guaranteed to jar your aesthetics into a new alignment and change the shape of things to come. If you're used to looking at the flowing lines of an M1935 or the bristling charm of an M1911, as we all were not long ago, a utilitarian Glock looks downright homely. But once you get used to looking at Glocks, older designs look, well, older.

Plenty of people took up Glocks even when they still thought they were ugly because, when form follows function, it's the function you fall in love with first. Aesthetic appreciation of the form of that function comes later, when

Liberty is for those who will settle for nothing less. Photo by the author.

you realize this is that rare thing you can trust with your life.

THE SECRET OF GLOCK'S SUCCESS

People fell in love with Glocks for the same reasons they first fell in love with 1911s—simplicity, trigger control, and balance. Glocks have only thirtysomething parts, the trigger pull is the same from one shot to the next, and the lightweight construction and Luger-like grip angle make the gun feel very much a part of your body. Glock outdid the 1911 and then kept going, offering unprecedented levels of strength, durability, and reliability possible only in a new age. Even more than the beloved cocked-and-locked 1911, the Glock pistol lives in a state of constant readiness.

Glocks have been widely copied but never

successfully so, because Glock remains very far ahead in the race. The introduction of the Austrian pistol is doubly significant in that it ended one revolution and began another.

The "wondernine" revolution, wherein complex high-capacity double-action 9mm pistols of German design origin unseated the stately American revolver from the hearts and minds of professionals throughout the country, ended abruptly when Gaston Glock introduced his "safe-action" pistols with their hard-hitting barrels and soft-recoiling frames. And the new revolution truly began when Austrian hardware and Americanized Swedish software merged in the first .40-caliber Glock.

For the first time in history, here was a light and fast-handling pistol capable of reliable sustained fire in a major man-stopping caliber. Such a weapon had never existed before.

Beauty is in the eye of the shooter. Photo by the author.

Virtually overnight, a sea change swept the ranks of handgunners. Double-action autos suddenly looked like the Rube Goldberg-type inventions they were. Chrome-plated, ivory-handled 1911s looked like display-case relics from a bygone age. Only the businesslike black plastic Glock pistol looked like it belonged in the hands of a serious shooter.

Professionals and novices alike were quickly drawn to the unique qualities of Glocks, and every major handgun manufacturer in the world was equally quick to follow in Glock's footsteps, producing guns with polymer components and long but consistent "double-action-only" trigger mechanisms. Smith & Wesson copied the Glock so slavishly it infringed on several Glock patents and paid the legal price for its offense. All of these companies somehow missed the point.

The secret of Glock's success is deceptively simple: Glock is the first semiautomatic pistol, in more than a hundred years of trying, to offer its owner the same comfort level as a revolver.

When you decide to fire, you pull the trigger. That's true love.

Even more than the beloved cocked-and-locked 1911, the Glock pistol lives in a state of constant readiness.

The Empty Chamber

19

If you drink red wine, you will eventually spill a drop on your clean white shirt. If you are a shooter, at some point in your shooting career you will pull the trigger on an empty chamber, hear a loud explosion as shock and disbelief quake your nervous system, and learn the most important lesson there is to learn about gunhandling.

A rigorous commitment to fundamental safety rules will make this astonishing "empty chamber" incident a harmless surprise, but it will happen nevertheless. You can count on it. Fate absolutely guarantees it. You must prepare yourself for it.

In many activities, basic safety rules are designed to protect amateurs from the common mistakes of inexperience. Professionals are expected to override these rules because of their higher level of competence. This is NOT the case in shooting.

Every professional knows full well that he is capable of making a mistake and that even the smallest mistake in shooting is a potentially lethal one. Only when he knows that the muzzle of his firearm is ALWAYS pointed in a truly SAFE direction can he be confident that his inevitable mistake will cause no permanent damage.

THERE ARE NO ACCIDENTS, ONLY NEGLIGENCE

Professionals refer to all "accidental discharges" by their real name—*negligent* discharges. There is no such thing as an accident in shooting, and there is no room in shooting for negligence. An injurious or lethal gun accident is the worst thing that could ever happen to a shooter and gun owner. Even a near miss can send you to a psychiatrist. And the consequences of your carelessness can easily be far worse than that.

It is for these reasons that I believe hunting is far better training for actually shooting somebody than playing with paintballs. When you point a gun at a living creature and see the graphic violent death that follows, the point is better made than with a water-soluble stain that washes out with a little Cheer.

It is not his capacity to reason or to speak, but his willingness to take responsibility for The Empty Chamber that separates man from the lower animals.

Exactly how empty is the chamber? Photo by the author.

The Constitutional Right and Social Obligation to Carry a Gun

20

There's an old wisecrack, true as witticisms, proverbs, and aphorisms usually are. It goes like this—*funny the things you see when you don't have a gun*. Suzanna Gratia (now Gratia Hupp) was having a pleasant lunch with her parents in Luby's cafeteria in Killeen, Texas, when she saw a pickup truck come crashing through the wall. A man armed with two guns and plenty of spare magazines emerged from the truck and started shooting everyone in sight, including Gratia's mother and father. Al Gratia was shot fatally in the chest. Ursula Gratia was shot point-blank in the head. More than 20 other people in the cafeteria were murdered in cold blood before the killer turned one of his guns on himself and blew his own brains out.

Suzanna hid under a table, clutching her purse, which normally contained a .38 revolver. In deference to Texas law at that time, which prohibited carrying concealed weapons on one's person, she had left her gun in her car. Several more dead diners had guns legally and inaccessibly locked in their cars. Suzanna Gratia Hupp has vowed never to make that mistake again, though such pronouncements always come far too late.

"The decision to follow the law cost me the lives of my parents," she says. "There is not a day that goes by when I do not think about that."

Not long after the Killeen massacre, John Taylor and Craig Godineaux knocked on the locked front door of a Wendy's restaurant in New York City. They called out to the

"The decision to follow the law cost me the lives of my parents."

manager, Jean Dumel Auguste, by name. Taylor was familiar with the operation and layout of the restaurant, having worked there for a short time before he was dismissed for theft. The manager opened the door for Taylor and Godineaux and led them to his basement office. Minutes later, he used the store's intercom to summon his entire night crew of six employees down into the basement for a meeting. What followed was one of the worst massacres in New York history.

The two armed killers herded all seven Wendy's employees into a walk-in refrigerator, bound their hands, gagged their mouths, covered their heads with plastic bags, ordered them to kneel on the floor, and methodically shot each person in the head with a small-caliber pistol at point-blank range. They then stole about $2,000 in cash and left. New York law and Wendy's corporate policy had prohibited the victims from arming themselves.

All of the people involved in these incidents were, in a profound way, responsible for their own deaths or the deaths of loved ones. They were equally responsible for the deaths of innocents who dared associate with them and, by abstract extension, for the deaths of everyone ever killed in similar circumstances. Antigun laws and policies are always complicit in the execution of innocents. And it's appropriate that survivors are always ashamed of their inadequacy.

In the final analysis, to face evil with impotence—whether out of cowardice or feeble-mindedness or submission to foolish laws—could well be responsible for the death of society.

Suzanna Gratia Hupp decided to fight back. She set out to change the foolish laws. She turned her anger on her legislators who had "legislated me out of the right to protect myself and my family." She joined the crusade for the right to carry concealed weapons in Texas, and she ran for the state legislature. She was successful on both counts, though not in time to save the lives of her parents.

Today, Rep. Hupp has some harsh words for those gun-control fanatics who come out of the woodwork every time there's a mass slaying like Columbine: "Why is it that mass shootings now seem to always take place in schools and post offices, places where guns are not allowed? They're always in these so-called gun-free safety zones." Like Luby's cafeteria.

Five Wendy's employees—Ramon Nazario, Anita C. Smith, Jeremy Mele, Ali Ibadat, and Jean Dumel Auguste—took their shame to their graves. There was no good reason on earth why it had to end that way.

A scenario almost identical to that of Wendy's in New York unfolded at Shoney's restaurant in Anniston, Alabama, in 1991. Two armed robbers took over the restaurant, which was filled with two dozen customers and several employees, and started to herd everyone into the restaurant's walk-in refrigerator. But this time a smart employee, Thomas Terry, drew his concealed .45 and shot both of the bad guys before this particular mass execution could take place. In a matter of seconds, one criminal lay dead, the other incapacitated, and more than two dozen innocent people had been handed back their lives thanks to a man who had a gun and was not afraid to use it. Thomas Terry, bleeding from a grazing wound to the hip, was happy to play the hero with so many lives at stake.

And still they ask, "Why do you carry a gun? What are you afraid of? Do you think some nut is going to drive through the wall and start shooting everybody? Do you think a couple of hardened criminals are going to shove you in the refrigerator and execute you?" To which you can only reply, "Do you think when you walk out of here and cross the street you're going to be hit by a truck?"

Only when the custom of carrying a gun once again achieves its deserved high level of social legitimacy and political priority will this country get back on the track of respect for human freedom and dignity that has set it apart from the rest of the world for two centuries.

THE ANTI-FREEDOM ZEALOTS

Ask any American and he'll tell you he believes in liberty. To a point, of course. All too often, when liberty goes beyond the inalienable right to choose one's own brand of mouthwash, the cold fear of freedom begins to seep into the bones.

Cheering on the fear of freedom are those quivering souls steeped in terror at the thought of independent decision-making and freedom of action on the part of their distrusted fellow man. These antifreedom zealots are members of the well-established international community of political ideologues who have brought you such gun-control activists as Joe Stalin and Chairman Mao. And since at least the 1930s it has been clear that even The Land of The Free has its share of these political low-lifes. We must face the fact that the antifreedom zealots have made their American home in the left, or "liberal," wing of today's Democratic Party.

Antifreedom zealots live in a wayward universe of their own making, a cosmos where nature is contradicted at every turn, where responses to every problem are suicidal measures as certain to make the problem worse as showering gasoline on a housefire. The upended logic of these fanatics is stunning: If there's a problem with bad guys shooting good guys, then let's make sure the good guys don't have guns.

Criminologist Cesare Beccaria, writing in the 18th century, had a word to say about antifreedom zealots" "False is the idea . . . that would take fire from men because it burns, and water because one may drown in it . . . The laws that forbid the carrying of arms are laws of such a nature. They disarm those only who are neither inclined nor determined to commit crimes. Can it be supposed that those who have the courage to violate the most sacred laws of humanity, the most important of the code, will respect the less important and arbitrary ones, which can be violated with ease and impunity, and which, if strictly obeyed, would put an end to personal liberty? Such laws make things worse for the assaulted and better for the assailants; they serve rather to encourage than to prevent homicides . . ."

Many Americans today have been taught by propaganda disseminated in the mass media that guns lead dangerous lives of their own. Thus the notorious antigun politician Rep. Henry Waxman (D-CA) describes a rare and highly desirable sporting rifle in the following terms: "This kind of weapon can blow up a limousine, a helicopter, can take out a vehicle, armored vehicle, maybe a mile away. It can shoot through seven buildings!"

One wonders why the rabid Mr. Waxman and his ilk don't use similar words to describe the lethal five-gallon bucket, an evil instrument of death which drowns twice as many children each year as are shot by America's 250 million guns.

Antifreedom zealots are both helpless and hopeless. They are like decaffeinated coffee, declawed cats, or poorly bred dogs who've been easily persuaded to forego their natural hunting instincts in order to avoid minor electrical shocks and so tend to have recurring problems with their weakened nervous systems.

Sarah Brady of Handgun Control Inc, has said, mimicking Clinton's pathetic duck-hunting argument, that "the only reason for guns in civilian hands is for sporting purposes." Antifreedom zealots like the Bradys and the Clintons need to be informed that to save one's life is not a sporting purpose. There's nothing sporting about it. If it takes a full battle-dress M16 or AK-47 to get the job done, well, that's what they're for.

In their terminal confusion, antifreedom zealots pay lip service to a Constitution they don't really understand, but in every act and every thought, whether out of total ignorance or deliberate intent, reveal that their mission is to facilitate the destruction of the Constitution and its replacement with an unnatural ideology most of us thought rusted to bloody dust a long time ago.

Anti-freedom zealots are a malignant danger to all life on Earth as we know it, because their anti-self-defense, antigun position is an expression of the most utter contempt for individual human life it is possible to conceive.

Antifreedom zealots need to be informed that to save one's life is not a sporting purpose. There's nothing sporting about it.

Antifreedom zealots see nothing wrong with leaning on their neighbors to provide them with personal protection even though they would never consider returning the favor. They worship their effeminate fantasy of an all-powerful government with true religious fanaticism. They believe all other humans are as mentally weak, irresponsible, incompetent and self-hating as they know themselves to be. And they encourage only civilization's most self-destructive tendencies.

To be charitable, anti-freedom zealots are unthinkingly naïve, stone-blind, and cowardly. To be frank, they are the evil seeds ultimately responsible for all the crime, war, and needless violence the planet has ever seen.

PARADISE LOST

In the beginning, weapons grew on trees.

In the lost paradise of our species, every man, woman, and child was armed to the teeth with the finest state-of-the-art killing machines society could produce, and all was well. As man grew more sophisticated and his weapons grew even more effective at protecting weaker citizens from stronger ones, the first evil caveman genius saw that, as a precursor to the enslavement and destruction of his intended victims, all who would dare resist him must first be disarmed. In the name of peace. In the name of social harmony. In the name of common sense. To save the children. Evil geniuses, and evil idiots, have been singing that tune ever since. And the more gullible among our species have all too often danced to it.

The now-dead Peter Shields, founder of the radical antigun Handgun Control Inc, sang, "If attacked, put up no defense. Give them what they want."

The aforementioned antigun politician, California Rep. Henry Waxman, sings, "If someone is so fearful that they're going to start using their weapons to protect their rights, it makes me very nervous that these people have these weapons at all!" Few politicians in today's unabashedly socialist Democratic Party have not at some time joined in the antigun chorus or made up worse verses of their own.

In the recent past, half of American voters demonstrated that they are capable of dancing to anything if it has a simple beat and a catchy tune. They cheerfully elected and reelected to the highest office in the land a psychopathic criminal and traitor of the lowest order, a thoroughly dishonest and evil man who devoted his entire personal and political life to the eradication of timeless human liberties Americans take for granted.

Few American voters have even read the Bill of Rights, brief as it is, much less understood its meaning and significance. How do you think they'd feel on any given day about a total rewrite? As the ghost of Bill Clinton fades back into the putrefied swamp from whence it came, we must remember the lessons learned.

Niccolò Machiavelli cautioned as early as the 16th century that the demise of the armed citizen meant the end of civic virtue and, with it, the end of the people's control over their own destiny—and a very fast end at that, as he observes in *The Art of War:* "Rome remained free for four hundred years and Sparta eight hundred, although their citizens were armed all that time; but many other states that have been disarmed have lost their liberties in less than forty years."

Whom are we to trust with our lives and our liberties, other than ourselves?

CARRYING A GUN IS
AN ABSOLUTE RIGHT

The framers of the Constitution were under no pressure from the NRA when they wrote, "The right of the people to keep and bear arms shall not be infringed."

In the same spare sentence, they reaffirmed their historical preference for a "militia" over a standing army, and indicated that this militia should be composed of armed citizens—citizens of a "free state" whose right to keep and bear arms must never be infringed. Antifreedom zealots, including academic invalids and the hypocrites of the misnamed American Civil Liberties Union, have stood on their pointy heads in tortured attempts to misinterpret this sentence ever since. Those of us who know how to read the English language have no trouble at all.

The right of the people to keep and bear arms shall not be infringed. THE RIGHT OF THE PEOPLE to keep and bear arms shall NOT be infringed. The right of the people TO KEEP AND BEAR ARMS shall NOT be infringed. The right of the people to keep and bear arms SHALL NOT BE INFRINGED. What part of NOT do the illiterates out to subvert the Constitution NOT understand?

The Constitution of the state of Pennsylvania (adopted September 28, 1776) allocated more words to make the point even more unmistakable: "XIII. That the people have a right to bear arms for the defence of themselves and the state; and as standing armies in the time of peace are dangerous to liberty, they ought not to be kept up; and that the military should be kept under strict subordination to, and governed by, the civil power."

Indeed, the individual right to keep and bear arms for personal defense is based on exactly the same principle as civilian control of the military. One wonders if the ACLU would argue with that.

The Second Amendment, like most other articles in the Bill of Rights, was adopted from the English Bill of Rights of 1689 which, in turn, was based on centuries of English Common Law. English jurist Sir William Blackstone observed that the English Bill of Rights clearly meant that Englishmen possessed "the right of having and using arms for self-preservation and defense" and that "having arms suitable for their defense" was one of the five auxiliary rights people possessed "to protect and maintain inviolate the three great and primary rights," the first of which is "personal security."

Unfortunately for the English people, they have been persuaded by their own far-left government and insidious antigun activists to allow the English Bill of Rights to be, as they might say, shat upon. Today, the English do not have the right to keep and bear arms for self-preservation and defense. As a direct result, they live in a crime-ridden society that grows worse with each passing day.

The recent 2000 International Crime Victims Survey published by the Dutch Ministry of Justice, a highly respected and accurate measurement of the percentage of people by nation who are victims of violent crimes, ranked England far ahead of the United States (which ranked 8th), and second only to Australia (where English-style antigun laws are also in effect) as the most violent nation. A recently disarmed England now has twice as much violent crime as the United States.

The English Home Office, which cooperated in the survey, has refused to publish these findings in England. It's better not to remind the gullible subjects how empty were the promises of safety and security for which they so eagerly traded away their very real and priceless freedoms and responsibilities.

The great Roman philosopher and senator, Cicero, immortalized armed self-defense as an "inalienable right" more than 2,000 years before the U.S. Constitution did so. Cicero said:

> There exists a law, not written down anywhere but inborn in our hearts; a law which comes to us not by training or custom or reading but by derivation and absorption and adoption from nature itself; a law which has come to us not from theory but from practice, not by instruction but by natural intuition. I refer to the law which lays it down that, if our lives are endangered by plots or violence or armed robbers or enemies, any and every method of protecting ourselves is morally right.

Niccolò Machiavelli cautioned that the demise of the armed citizen meant the end of civic virtue.

Even people to whom armed self-defense is but a remote abstraction often endorse, without even realizing it, the unquestionable principles underlying the right to carry a gun. Jaron Lanier, writing in *Discover Magazine* (February 2001) said in reference to new copyright-protection technology, "In a democracy, citizens are supposed to act as partners in enforcing laws. Those forced to follow rules without being trusted even for a moment are, in fact, slaves."

It is perfectly obvious that we have a natural right to arm ourselves and to kill any criminal or other force that threatens us just as surely as an elephant has a right to kill an attacking lion and a mother bear has a right to kill a wolf grinning suspiciously at her cubs. Animal-rights extremists extend the animals' right to the killing of humans under such circumstances.

Even the Dalai Lama, Nobel Peace Prize and all, said in May 2001 during a speech about "nonviolent resolutions to conflict" to 7,600 Oregon and Washington high-school students, "But if someone has a gun and is trying to kill you, it would be reasonable to shoot back with your own gun." So said the Dalai Lama.

There are criminals among us who are both homicidal and incorrigible. Their parents took a shot at civilizing them and failed. Their schoolteachers took a shot at them and failed. The odds are overwhelming that government welfare programs and penal institutions took a shot at them and failed. If it ever becomes your turn to take a shot at them, don't fail.

CARRYING A GUN HAS ALWAYS BEEN BOTH A RIGHT AND A DUTY

There have been many societies in which *not* carrying a weapon was a serious and severely punishable crime. This was true in Greece, Rome, Europe, and Britain and, though seldom enforced, is still true in certain places in America

today. This is as it should be. A citizen who shirks his duty to contribute to the security of his community is little better than the criminal who threatens it, and is better off living in a society that places lesser demands on his capacity to accept responsibility. As cowards from the Vietnam era discovered, that's what Canada is for.

English scholar Granville Sharpe, who helped bring about the abolition of slavery in England and supported American independence, wrote in 1782 that "No Englishman can be truly loyal who opposes the principles of English law whereby the people are required to have arms of defence and peace, for mutual as well as private defence. . . . The laws of England always required the people to be armed, and not only armed, but to be expert in arms."

In 1785, William Blizard, chief legal advisor to London's mayor and city council, stated that "The right of his majesty's Protestant subjects, to have arms for their own defence, and to use them for lawful purposes, is most clear and undeniable. It seems, indeed, to be considered, by the ancient laws of this kingdom, not only as a right, but as a *duty* . . ."

Commenting on the early legal requirement that every American male and every American household be armed, attorney Don B. Kates says that citizens "were not simply *allowed* to keep their own arms, but affirmatively *required* to do so." He further says that these statutes reflect the classical world view that "arms possession for protection of self, family, and polity was both the hallmark of the individual's freedom and one of the two primary factors in his developing the independent, self-reliant, responsible character which classical political philosophers deemed necessary to the citizenry of a free state."

You don't have to have lived in ancient Greece or Rome or Middle Ages England or revolutionary America or on the west side of L.A.

The more guns there are in society and the more these guns are carried by private citizens, the less crime there is.

during the Manson massacres, as I did, to know that anyone who lives in a house without a gun is a dangerous fool.

There have not always been police. England had none until 1829, America had none until 1845, and only in the so-called modern era have police officers been armed. At one time, fear of anything resembling a standing army was so intense that police were, in fact, the only citizens *not* allowed to carry guns. Throughout much of 19th century England and America, the policy of forbidding police to have arms while on duty was the *only* form of gun control.

Police were expected to rely on a fully armed citizenry to come to their aid when armed enforcement of the law was necessary—a circumstance that occurs with growing regularity today.

ARMED CITIZENS OF THE 21ST CENTURY

On January 3, 2001, the Citizens' Self-Defense Act of 2001, intended "to protect the right to obtain firearms for security and to use firearms in defense of self, family, or home, and to provide for the enforcement of such right" was introduced in the U.S. House of Representatives. Given the current sorry state of our elected representatives, the bill was never expected to pass into law, but rather to serve as a symbol of just how timid, disconnected from reality, and contemptuous of liberty most Washington politicians—who would never consider voting for such a bill—have become.

It doesn't matter. The fundamental liberties reaffirmed in H.R. 31 were never granted by politicians in the first place. The source of these liberties is as old as the first free man. And, as long as man is free, the source will remain.

Included in the Citizens' Self-Defense Act of 2001 are the following Congressional findings:

(1) Police cannot protect, and are not legally liable for failing to protect, individual citizens, as evidenced by the following:

  (A) The courts have consistently ruled that the police do not have an obligation to protect individuals, only the public in general. For example, in Warren v. District of Columbia Metropolitan Police Department, 444 A.2d 1 (D.C. App. 1981), the court stated: "[C]ourts have without exception concluded that when a municipality or other governmental entity undertakes to furnish police services, it assumes a duty only to the public at large and not to individual members of the community."

  (B) Former Florida Attorney General Jim Smith told Florida legislators that police responded to only 200,000 of 700,000 calls for help to Dade County authorities.

  (C) The United States Department of Justice found that, in 1989, there were 168,881 crimes of violence for which police had not responded within one hour.

  (D) Currently, there are about 150,000 police officers on duty at any one time.

(2) Citizens frequently must use firearms to defend themselves, as evidenced by the following:

  (A) Every year, more than 2,400,000 people in the United States use a gun to defend themselves against criminals—or more than 6,500 people a day. This means that, each year, firearms are used 60 times more often to protect the lives of honest citizens than to take lives.

  (B) Of the 2,400,000 self-defense cases, more than 192,000 are by women defending themselves against sexual abuse.

(C) Of the 2,400,000 times citizens use their guns to defend themselves every year, 92 percent merely brandish their gun or fire a warning shot to scare off their attackers. Less than eight percent of the time does a citizen kill or wound his or her attacker.

(3) Law-abiding citizens, seeking only to provide for their families' defense, are routinely prosecuted for brandishing or using a firearm in self-defense. For example:

(A) In 1986, Don Bennett of Oak Park, Illinois, was shot at by two men who had just stolen $1,200 in cash and jewelry from his suburban Chicago service station. The police arrested Bennett for violating Oak Park's handgun ban. The police never caught the actual criminals.

(B) Ronald Biggs, a resident of Goldsboro, North Carolina, was arrested for shooting an intruder in 1990. Four men broke into Biggs' residence one night, ransacked the home and then assaulted him with a baseball bat. When Biggs attempted to escape through the back door, the group chased him and Biggs turned and shot one of the assailants in the stomach. Biggs was arrested and charged with assault with a deadly weapon—a felony. His assailants were charged with misdemeanors.

(C) Don Campbell of Port Huron, Michigan, was arrested, jailed, and criminally charged after he shot a criminal assailant in 1991. The thief had broken into Campbell's store and attacked him. The prosecutor plea-bargained with the assailant and planned to use him to testify against Campbell for felonious use of a firearm. Only after intense community pressure did the prosecutor finally drop the charges.

(4) The courts have granted immunity from prosecution to police officers who use firearms in the line of duty. Similarly, law-abiding citizens who use firearms to protect themselves, their families, and their homes against violent felons should not be subject to lawsuits by the violent felons who sought to victimize them.

In 1987, a year after Glocks were introduced to the United States, Florida enacted a pioneering "shall-issue" right-to-carry law that has served as the model for the rest of the country. The Florida law affirmed the right of a private citizen to carry a concealed gun and eliminated the abuses so typical of "discretionary" right-to-carry laws that resulted in gun permits being awarded arbitrarily to the political cronies of petty officials, limousine liberals, movie actors, athletes, and various other celebrity representatives of the rich and famous crowd, but denied to so-called "ordinary" citizens. The Florida law made it crystal clear that any citizen with basic firearms training and a felony-free record would be issued a concealed-carry permit upon request, period.

Florida's landmark right-to-carry law was supported by the Florida Department of Law Enforcement, Florida Sheriffs Association, Florida Police Chiefs Association, and other law enforcement groups. And it was supported by Florida voters.

The media, however, was predictably vociferous in its opposition to the exercise of Constitutionally guaranteed rights and in its total submission to the party line of radical antifreedom, anti-self-defense and antigun forces. Headlines predicted vigilante justice and wild-west shootouts on every corner. "Florida will become the "Gunshine State." "A pistol-packing citizenry will mean itchier trigger fingers." "Florida's climate of smoldering fear will flash like napalm when every stranger totes a piece." "Every mental snap in traffic could lead to the crack of gunfire."

Such dire and colorful predictions, of course, proved totally false. Nevertheless, that same hysterical fear-mongering and bald-faced lying are used even today every time a new state gets ready to pass an enlightened right-to-carry law. In actual fact, the only notable thing that happened for the first five years after Florida passed its right-to-carry law was that, as homicide rates in the United States soared, Florida's homicide rate fell a dramatic 23 percent. A few of the opponents of concealed carry actually had the courage to admit they were wrong.

Thanks to the intensive lobbying efforts of the NRA, along with the tireless grassroots work of politically aware gunowners, 33 states now have Florida-style laws that require the prompt issuance to their citizens of legal permits to carry concealed weapons. Well over half of the U.S. population, more than 60 percent of all handgun owners, live in these free states, yet no more than one to five percent ever apply for such licenses.

Notwithstanding the fact that most people do not carry guns, the mere possibility that an intended victim could be armed with a handgun eliminates millions of crimes every year.

According to the FBI, states with "shall-issue" right-to-carry laws enjoy an average of 26-percent lower total violent crime rate, 20-percent lower homicide rate, 39-percent lower robbery rate, and 22-percent lower aggravated assault rate than those states that do not allow their citizens to carry guns legally.

Florida State University Professor of Criminology and Criminal Justice Gary Kleck, in *Point Blank: Guns and Violence in America* (Aldine de Gruyter Publishers 1991), found that "robbery and assault victims who used a gun to resist were less likely to be attacked or to suffer an injury than those who used any other methods of self-protection or those who did not resist at all."

Kleck points to surveys confirming the fact that convicted felons are more afraid of armed citizens than they are of the police. And well they

should be. According to Kleck's research, armed citizens kill 2,000 to 3,000 criminals each year, three times the number killed by the police. And only 2 percent of civilian shootings involve an innocent person mistakenly identified as a criminal, whereas the error rate for the police is more than five times that high.

Kleck's research shows that private citizens use firearms to protect themselves and thwart crime about 2.5 million times a year. Citizens use firearms to prevent mass killings, bank robberies, gang attacks, carjackings, rapes, kidnappings and hostage-takings. They use them to help capture prison escapees and murderers, to come to the aid of outnumbered or ambushed law enforcement officers. Yet only a handful of these 2.5 million life-saving uses of firearms are ever reported in the mainstream press.

If a lot more people carried guns, what kind of a society would we have? Certainly not the kind predicted by antigun fanatics. Those hysterical doomsayers have been proven absolutely wrong 100 percent of the time. Would we have a crime-free society? Certainly not. Criminals are as natural and immune to total eradication as fruit flies. But a better-armed society would severely limit the violent damage criminals wreak before they are stopped. Criminals are naturally self-destructive. The reasons they are so doesn't matter. To assist them in their self-destructiveness is the polite and civilized thing to do. Thus another ageless axiom: An Armed Society Is a Polite Society.

In his essay, *Behavior Modification and Self Defense*, Michael Mitchell writes,

> Laws do one thing and one thing only—provide a penalty for wrongful

The only notable thing that happened for the first five years after Florida passed its right-to-carry law was that its homicide rate dropped a dramatic 23 percent.

behavior. The function of laws is to punish people, and punishment is a form of behavior modification. But laws are obviously only effective on the law-abiding populace. Criminals, by definition, don't respect the law; they make their living breaking it. And fear of punishment is only effective if it is swift, sure, and severe.

In these days when the legal system cannot be relied upon to provide effective punishment for criminal behavior, armed self-defense can. It's definitely swift, as the gun will appear during or immediately after the negative behavior. It's sure, since, if the criminal doesn't stop his assault, he will be shot. And most people would definitely call a bullet to the chest severe.

The beauty of armed self-defense is that, because of its immediate, sure, and severe nature, the mere threat is usually enough to stop the behavior. Is it any wonder that states that pass concealed-carry laws experience immediate and obvious drops in crime rates? The violent criminal in these states isn't nearly as worried about being arrested for his crime as he is about being shot by his would-be victim. This fact fits perfectly with well-established principles of behavior modification.

On the flip side, the crime facilitators (gun control advocates), with their notions that we should submit to criminal assault, reward criminal behavior. The criminal gets what he wants—your money, your dignity, and maybe your life. Since positive reinforcement—reward—is the strongest, most effective behavior modification tool, that criminal behavior is likely to be repeated. In other words, by submitting to criminal demands, you are encouraging criminal behavior.

Mitchell did not say, but I will, that the most effective way to modify the behavior of a criminal is to modify it to the extent that he is no longer capable of any behavior at all.

In 1998, John R. Lott Jr., senior research scholar in the School of Law at Yale University, authored the most comprehensive and exhaustive study of crime and gun control laws ever conceived, based on the largest data set on crime ever assembled, from the files of the FBI and other federal government agencies, state law enforcement agencies, county sheriffs, district attorneys, and more. His landmark book, *More Guns, Less Crime* (The University of Chicago Press, 1998, 2000), now available in an updated second edition, includes thorough analyses of more than 54,000 observations and hundreds of variable factors across more than 3,000 counties in all 50 states for 18 years.

The assiduously researched conclusions reached by Lott immediately set off a wave of panic among antigun fanatics and drew organized, systematic personal attacks of the most vicious and dishonest nature, including death threats leveled at Lott and his wife and children. Yet not a single serious academic challenge of Lott's research, his methodology, or his incontrovertible conclusions has ever been mounted successfully. In fact, even a few established icons of the liberal mainstream press have reluctantly called Lott's conclusions "bulletproof." Among those conclusions are the following:

- Gun ownership saves lives.
- Gun ownership also saves money. Nationwide, each one-percent increase in the number of people owning guns reduces crime victim costs by more than $3 billion.
- Concealed handgun carry by private citizens

Police support right-to-carry laws for private citizens by an overwhelming three-to-one margin.

reduces violent crimes, including rape, murder, aggravated assault, and robbery, throughout the entire community and in surrounding communities.

- When a state passes a right-to-carry law, crime reduction is immediate and substantial, and crime-reduction benefits continue to grow the longer the law is in effect.
- The greater the number of concealed handgun permits issued, the greater the reduction in crime.
- Mass shootings in public places are reduced to virtually zero within four or five years after right-to-carry laws are passed—except in designated "gun-free" zones, such as schools, where self-defense is known to be prohibited.
- The largest drops in violent crime from concealed handgun carry occur in the most urban areas with the greatest populations and the highest crime rates.
- Citizens who do not carry guns benefit equally from the crime reduction that results when other citizens carry guns. The people who benefit most from this "halo" effect are women, children, the elderly, and blacks.
- Of all the methods studied by economists, the carrying of concealed handguns is by far the most cost-effective method for reducing crime. Each and every concealed handgun permit issued reduces total economic losses to crime victims by $3,000 to $5,000.
- Accident and suicide rates are unaltered by the presence of concealed handguns.
- The effect of increased penalties for using a gun in the commission of a crime is small.
- The Brady Law, other mandated waiting periods, safe-storage laws, and one-gun-a-month laws all increase crime, especially rape.
- Background checks, training requirements, and age restrictions have no crime-reduction benefits.
- Bottom line, in keeping with the title of his work, the more guns there are in society and the more these guns are carried by private citizens, the less crime there is.

These are some of the reasons police, who fight crime for a living and are well aware of the realities of street criminals, support right-to-carry laws for private citizens by an overwhelming three-to-one margin. This is an even higher margin of support for right-to-carry than the strong support voiced by the civilian population.

Policemen are nobody's personal bodyguards. Their jobs are to find and arrest people who have committed crimes, not to prevent such potential crimes from happening in the first place. Clearly, the responsibility for victim-prevention lies with the victim-to-be.

The Seventh Circuit Court of Appeals (*Bowers v. DeVito,* 1982) did not mince words when it ruled, "There is no Constitutional right to be protected by the state against being murdered by criminals or madmen."

WHAT IT MEANS TO CARRY A GUN

That loaded Glock in your holster is a powerful expression of your Constitutionally guaranteed liberty as an American citizen, your recognition of the solemn duty you have to your fellow man, and your willingness to accept the full weight of a life-and-death responsibility.

When you are prepared to defend yourself, you are equally prepared to defend all of society and all of its guiding principles. Your responsibilities are therefore many—moral, legal, and tactical. That is why most people, including lifelong gunowners, experienced hunters, and competitive shooters, even in states that freely issue concealed carry permits, do not choose to carry a gun.

Your moral responsibilities are to fire your gun into another human being only when the line of necessity has clearly been reached, and then to fire without hesitation and to full effect. Remember the words of Cicero.

Your legal responsibilities are to justify your actions to those who would call you a criminal at the drop of a hat, and quite possibly to a jury of your peers, most of whom have neither the competence nor the courage to carry a gun in their own defense. Read the findings of the Citizens' Self-Defense Act of 2001.

Your tactical responsibilities are to carry your

To face evil with impotence could well be responsible for the death of society.

gun with confidence, to be well trained in your ability to operate it effectively, and to have instilled in yourself an iron will to use deadly force to prevent or end violence against yourself or others. Most of this book is dedicated to your tactical responsibilities, because that's what will save your life.

Violence either happens at random, is directed toward the obviously vulnerable, or is directed toward someone in particular for a reason. You can rest assured it will not happen at the shooting range when you are all suited up in your speed rig with a plan of action worked out for the coming run-and-gun stage. It will happen when you are home sleeping in your bed, shopping at the grocery store, walking out to get the mail, mowing the grass, at dinner, at church, at the theater.

The most dangerous places in the world are those called "gun-free safety zones" by their ignorant political creators and known by criminals and psychopaths as "safe-to-kill zones." Even an adolescent school kid can figure out that an advertised killing field where no one is allowed to shoot back is the safest location in the world to carry out a mass shooting. Don't even consider going to a place like that unarmed, whether it's your kid's school or a national park. If you can't handle breaking the law, don't go.

The assistant principal of a high school in Pearl, Mississippi, broke the law. He kept a .45 in his car parked on the school grounds. When a deranged student opened fire, Joel Myrick ran for his gun. Two students were killed because Myrick had to retrieve his gun from his car instead of his holster. But the .45 eventually prevailed, and Myrick stopped the massacre long before police arrived on the scene. God only knows how many lives he saved. But assistant principal Joel Myrick wasn't awarded any medals. Of the several hundred newspaper and television stories about the incident, only a few even mentioned his

name. Almost none revealed the fact that he used a gun to stop the killings.

When you bodyguard someone for a while, or when you just live a normal life with your eyes wide open, you realize how vulnerable we all are to becoming another tidbit-of-opportunity in the relentless food chain that sustains the life of this unpredictable world. It's a realization not of paranoia but of reality. That's the way it is, always has been, always will be. You can ignore it out of faint-heartedness, deny it out of lunacy, submit to it out of a fatalistic contempt for your own life and the lives of others, or you can face it with courage and intelligence and prepare yourself to deal with capricious reality's predisposition toward danger.

Most of those dangers can be met with nothing more than a strong I'm-not-a-victim mind-set and body language. Many others may shrivel with the demonstration of superior verbal skills. Still others may require a fundamental knowledge of martial arts, a container of pepper spray, a makeshift club, the presence of a well-wielded knife, or the sight of a firearm. A few, perhaps one in a lifetime, will not be affected by any kind of less-than-lethal response and will not end until you churn your attacker's dreams and determination into a chunky red stew and spew it all over the street with a couple of big-bore hollowpoints. The trouble is, you never know when or where that last one is coming.

If you ever find yourself under attack by an armed criminal, you will be on the defensive and he will be on the offensive. In other words, he will have a strong advantage going in. And, though he will not have trained himself to shoot nearly as well as you have trained, he will be far more experienced in the art of killing. The odds are, any criminal who is intent on killing you has probably killed men before, knows how to do it, knows how it feels, and likes it. You're not going to talk him out of it, scare him out of it, or wound him out of it. You're going to have to kill him.

Studies show that simply brandishing a weapon saves many lives, but I am personally against the idea of waving a gun around while your adversary thinks. The way to overcome his offensive advantage is to strike without warning. Once you make the decision to free your Glock from its holster the entire situation should be over and done with in a second or two. The most important component in practicing your draw is firing the instant you have a sight picture on your target—and continuing to fire until your assailant no longer exists.

More than a century of military and police research tells us that most people, including up to 85 percent of trained soldiers and cops, are psychologically unable to use deadly force in a life-or-death situation no matter how compelling the circumstances may be. If you can't kill, there is no reason for you to carry a lethal weapon.

Carrying a loaded gun with the ability and will to use it is not a casual fling meant to bring some excitement into your boring life. It is an all-embracing lifestyle and must take precedence over your respect for law, your fear of social criticism, your love of humanity, your wardrobe, and your drinking habits.

You can never be unaware of the weight you carry on your hip or under your arm. You can never forget your responsibilities. You must wear your Glock with the same allegiance as your wedding ring. If you're not married, your Glock *is* your wedding ring. Wear it for life. Don't even think about leaving home without it. Be prepared to use it at a moment's notice. Carry it all the time. And shoot to kill.

"Liberty or death," the meaning of which is clear and absolute, is but a trivial phrase if you do not carry a gun. For freedom-loving Americans, the five most important words in the English language are, and always have been, *from my cold dead hands.*

Parting Shots

21

Strong Constitution

Mike Rose earns his living getting pro-Second-Amendment politicians elected and keeping them elected. His personal carry gun is a Glock 27, but he takes his hard-kicking G29 out for some mutual exercise at every opportunity. Photo by the author.

"I've never met a Glock I didn't like. Between myself and all my Glock friends, I've fired every Glock ever made. If I could manage it, I'd carry one of each all the time."

Le Femme Sonja

Fashion model Sonja Hawley shows us true feminine style. Photo by the author.

"Glocks are a girl's best friend."

Shooting the Shooters

Morgan W. Boatman, director of the videotape production of The Great Glock Watermelon Shoot, finally got his turn behind the trigger. Photo by the author.

"Got any more ammo?"

Glock Family Values

Chad Hyslop is an up-and-coming gun writer and the former press secretary for a U.S. Congressman. Chad is built to conceal a big 10mm Glock 20 in his waistband, and his wife Courtney backs him up with a Glock 19. Photo by the author.

"My kids are at the stage where they crawl all over you. At first, I thought I wouldn't carry my Glock when we were just relaxing like that. Then I realized that when I'm with the kids is the most important time to be armed. Besides, the best way to teach your kids safety is not to lock up your gun but to wear it."

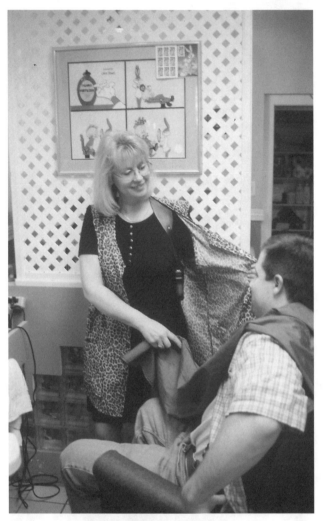

I'll Show You Mine if You Show Me Yours

Gussie O'Connor is barber to the political stars of Idaho's capital city and the mayor of a suburban Boise city herself. Here she compares precision instruments with a regular customer. Photo by the author.

"When I was first elected mayor, the county sheriff insisted that I carry a gun. I resisted at first, but now it's second nature. The little Glock 26 is more comfortable to wear all day than my cell phone."

Smoke This!

Mark Sturman, owner of the author's favorite cigar store, has two extracurricular passions—one of which he's sitting on and one of which is riding on his strong side. Photo by the author.

"The good things in life and the simple things in life are often the same."

Soft-Boiled Private Eye

Ms. Terre Lee is a private detective who doesn't always carry a gun. But when she does . . . Photo by the author.

"All my cop friends, both private and public, insist that I carry a Glock."

Father and Son

Political advisor Graham Paterson and his 12-year-old son Andrew share a memorable moment in the desert. Photo by the author.

"It's important for kids to learn about guns as early as possible. When Andrew graduated from a .22 to a .40-caliber Glock it was exciting for both of us."

Family Business

Jerry Sweet is president of one of the largest and oldest family-owned chains of sporting gooods stores in the Northwest. The Sweet family has hunted game all over the world. Photo by the author.

"Handgun hunting is one of the fastest-growing Glock sports."

Field Gun

Political consultant, advertising agency owner, and inveterate bird hunter Pat Reilly never takes to the field without his trusty companions. Photo by the author.

"In the fields of hunting, advertising, and politics, you've got to be prepared for the unexpected."

Starsky or Hutch?

Hollywood screenwriter Bill Keys has done his best to keep a generation of TV and movie cops well armed and tactically correct. Photo by the author.

"In real life, cops are seldom there when and where you need them. Anyone who ventures into the unknown without a man-stopper in his pocket is a fool."

Men in Black & White

Author and son, writer/filmmaker Morgan W. Boatman, see eye-to-eye on the things that count—like words and hats and plastic pistols. Photo by Laura Lawson Boatman.

"A Glock is a Glock is a Glock."

End of Days

Soldier of Fortune takes a break after another thousand-round weekend. Photo by Mike Rose.

"Mike, did you bring the Guinness?"

Lady Liberty

Sculptor Auguste Bartholdi should have thought of this. Thanks to Galco for the holster and the bright idea, and to Richard Sanwich for the execution.

"The right of the people to keep and bear arms shall not be infringed."

Afterword:
Tell Me a Story

There are 8 million stories in the Glock world. Stories about the black pistol in action defending the innocent, fighting crime, preventing tragedy, saving lives. Stories about sporting Glocks in the hunting field and on the competition course. Concealed carry stories. War stories. Cop stories. Individual achievement stories. Family stories. Funny stories. Overheard stories.

Still forming in the electronic brain of my word processor is a book devoted to these stories, whether serious or lighthearted, made of gritty reality or the stuff of legends. If you have any Glock stories to tell, please let me know. I can be reached through Paladin Press, directly via e-mail at interboat@aol.com, or at my Web site: *www.livingwithglocks.com*.

-rhb

P.S.
11-Sept-01

Carrying a gun has been returned to its ancient and rightful status, not only as a common-sense custom to ensure safety of self and loved ones, but as an essential element of national security.

Let's roll.

Index

Living with Glocks